CW00522178

TUTOR TO THE DRAGON EMPEROR

Reginald Fleming Johnston in his Ch'ing coat; he is dressed as a court official of the First Degree. (By kind permission of the Merchant Company of Edinburgh and the Governing Council of George Watson's College, Edinburgh)

TUTOR TO THE DRAGON EMPEROR

THE LIFE OF SIR REGINALD FLEMING JOHNSTON AT THE COURT OF THE LAST EMPEROR OF CHINA

RAYMOND LAMONT-BROWN

SUTTON PUBLISHING

First published in 1999 by
Sutton Publishing Limited · Phoenix Mill
Thrupp · Stroud · Gloucestershire · GL5 2BU

British Library Cataloguing in Publication Data
A catalogue record for this book is available from the British Library

ISBN 0-7509-2106-4

Title-page calligraphy: a *fu* (charm) collected by Reginald Fleming Johnston at Weiheiwei 'to throw a whole army of demons into helpless confusion'.

(*Lion and Dragon in Northern China*, 1910)

Typeset in 11.5/16pt Bembo Mono.
Typesetting and origination by
Sutton Publishing Limited.
Printed in Great Britain by
Biddles, Guildford, Surrey.

CONTENTS

ACKNOWLEDGEMENTS

After the death of Sir Reginald Fleming Johnston on 6 March 1938, and in accordance with his verbal wishes to his sole residuary legatee and literary beneficiary Mrs Elizabeth Sparshott, his letters, papers and personal archives at Eilean Righ were destroyed. Thus the piecing together of the famous sinologist's biography has been an uphill task. Vital assistance has been given to the author in this work by the following.

A very special thank-you goes to Mr A.M. Young, partner in the law firm of J. & R.A. Robertson WS, Edinburgh, for generously locating, and opening for perusal, the correspondence files relating to Sir Reginald. Other important assistance in tracing documents, photographs and relevant data is gratefully acknowledged to: Professor Hugh D.R. Baker, Dept of East Asia Studies, School of Oriental and African Studies, University of London; I.C. Cunningham, Keeper of Manuscripts, National Library of Scotland; Dr Murray Simpson, Sub-Librarian and Arnott T. Wilson, University Archivist, Edinburgh University Library; Simon Bailey, Archivist, Oxford University Archives; John Alexander McGowan, Records Dept, The Law Society of Scotland; C.V.G. Harries, Senior Assistant Registrar, University of Bristol; Andrew Bethune, Edinburgh Room, Edinburgh City Libraries; Dr Robin Darwall-Smith, Archivist, Magdalen College, Oxford; Helen Langley, Modern Political Papers Reading Room, Dept of Western Manuscripts, Bodleian Library, Oxford; Mrs W. Poynton, Librarian, The Incorporated Society for Psychical Research;

Andrew Farthing, Local History Unit, Southport Library; Dr Raymond Refausse, Librarian and Archivist, Representative Church Body Library, Church of Ireland; Veronica Steel, Royal Commission on the Ancient and Historical Monuments of Scotland; Very Revd D. Cecil Orr; Caroline Oates, Assistant Librarian, Folklore Society; Martin Beckett, State Library, New South Wales; Jack Davis, Glasgow Libraries; Robert N. Andersen, Rensselaer County Historical Society, Troy, New York; Zoe Lubowiecka, Hove Reference Library; Dr Frances Wood, Chinese Section, British Library; and Mrs M. Cavedaschi, British Newspaper Library. Important fieldwork was also carried out by Margeorie Mekie, Bill Ellis and Charles J. Smith.

Advice on rights and permissions has been gratefully received from Iona Maclellan at Victor Gollancz and Deborah Gill at John Murray. Particular thanks go to Victor Gollancz and copyright holders Dr James and Mr Michael Pitt-Payne for permission to quote from Johnston's *Twilight in the Forbidden City*. A sight of original research on Johnston by Mrs Sarah Markham and Dr Robert Bickers is also acknowledged.

All photographs are acknowledged in situ, but individual help in tracing some images was given by Professor Maxine Berg, University of Warwick, and Simon Wilson, Assistant Archivist, School of Oriental and African Studies, University of London.

Chronology of the Main Events in the Lives of Reginald Fleming Johnston and Emperor Pu Yi

1874	*13 October* Johnston born at Morningside, Edinburgh
1879	Johnston enters Strathmore House Preparatory School, Southport
1881	Johnston enters Falcon Hall School, Morningside, Edinburgh
1890	Johnston begins work at his father's law office
1892	Johnston matriculates at University of Edinburgh
1898	*20 October* Johnston graduates BA(Oxon), University of Oxford
	Enters himself for Indian Civil Service Examination; he is offered and accepts a 'cadetship' in Colonial Service at Hong Kong
	25 December Johnston arrives at Hong Kong in the year Britain obtains lease of Weiheiwei
1899	Johnston is appointed Acting Clerk to the Administrative Councils, and Assistant Colonial Secretary, Hong Kong
	Boxer attacks on Christians, and foreign operations, begin at Shantung

Chronology

1900–2	Johnston serves as Private Secretary to Sir Henry Blake, Governor of Hong Kong
1901	*25 July* Johnston meets Pu Yi's father Prince Ch'un for the first time at Hong Kong
	Boxer terrorism ceases with allied signing of Boxer Protocol
1902	Johnston's first expedition into the hinterland of China
1904	*9/10 February–5 September 1905* Russo-Japanese War
	Johnston takes up post at Weiheiwei, and begins to write about environs of new posting
	Johnston becomes Southern District Magistrate, Weiheiwei
1906	*6 January–5 October* Second main trip to Chinese hinterland
	7 February Birth of Emperor Aisin-Gioro Pu Yi
1908	*14 November* Death of Emperor Kuang-hsu
	15 November Death of Empress Dowager Tzu Hsi
	2 December Pu Yi enthroned as the Hsuan-T'ung Emperor
1911	Republican revolution in China led by Dr Sun Yat-sen
	Johnston falls in love with Alice Walter, and publishes his anti-missionary book under a Chinese soubriquet
1912	*1 January* Republic of China proclaimed
	12 February Pu Yi abdicates
	15 February General Yuan Shih-k'ai becomes provisional president of China
1916	*13 April* Death of General Yuan Shih-k'ai
1917	*1 July* Revolt in Chinese army; Pu Yi restored as Emperor
	8 July Revolt vanquished. Pu Yi abdicates once more
1919	*22 February* Johnston takes up position as tutor to Pu Yi, and acquires retreat in Western Hills which he calls Cherry Glen
1922	*1 December* Pu Yi marries Wan Jung (Beautiful Countenance). Johnston is an honoured guest
1924	*5 November* Imperial Family is ordered to quit the Forbidden City. Pu Yi decamps to his father's house, the Northern Mansion
	29 November Johnston arranges Pu Yi's flight to Japanese Legation, Peking

CHRONOLOGY

1925	*23 February* Pu Yi arrives in Japanese-occupied Tientsin
1926	Johnston is appointed Secretary to British China Indemnity Delegation
1927	Chiang Kai-shek forms National Government at Nanking
	Civil war breaks out between Nationalists and Communists
	Johnston is appointed British Commissioner at Weiheiwei
1929	Johnston falls in love with Eileen Power
1930	*September* Johnston visits Pu Yi at Tientsin
	10 October Johnston returns to Britain and is knighted
1931	*3 March* Johnston is appointed to Chair of Chinese Studies, School of Oriental Studies, University of London
	Proposed marriage to Eileen Power is abandoned
	September Imperial Japanese Army invades Manchuria
	October Johnston is in Tientsin with Pu Yi. Johnston is involved in the Pacific Conference and Boxer Indemnity Business
	10 November Supported by Japanese Military Intelligence agents, Pu Yi is taken to Manchuria
1932	*23 February* Pu Yi is appointed Chief Executive of the new Japanese Protectorate of Manchuquo
1934	*1 March* Pu Yi is enthroned as puppet Emperor of Manchuquo
	8 October Johnston buys islands including Eilean Righ, Scotland
1935	*April* Pu Yi makes state visit to Japan
	May Johnston visits Pu Yi
1937	*29 June* Johnston retires from Chair of Chinese and goes to live at Eilean Righ with Elizabeth Sparshott
	7 July Japan invades China
1938	*6 March* Death of Reginald Fleming Johnston
1940	*September* Japan joins Axis powers, Germany and Italy
1941	*7 December* Japanese aircraft attack Pearl Harbor at 7.53 am local time
	8 December Japan declares war on USA and Great Britain

1942 *15 February* Fall of Singapore. Pu Yi pledges support of Japanese militarism through Manchuquo administration

1945 *6 August* Atomic bomb is dropped on Hiroshima, Japan
8 August Russia declares war on Japan; invades Manchuquo
9 August Atomic bomb is dropped on Nagasaki
15 August Pu Yi flees to Korean border and abdicates
17 August Pu Yi attempts to escape Soviet capture by going to Japan; seized by Soviets

1946 *August* Pu Yi gives evidence at War Crimes Trial; he vilifies Johnston

1949 *1 October* Mao Tse-tung proclaims 'People's Republic of China'

1950 *31 July* Soviets return Pu Yi to China; he is incarcerated in former Japanese prison at Fushun

1959 Pu Yi completes Communist brainwashing programme
September Pu Yi receives 'Special Pardon' and returns to Peking; visits Forbidden City. Begins ghostwritten autobiography which further vilifies and ridicules Johnston

1962 *1 May* Pu Yi marries Li Shusien

1967 *17 October* Death of Pu Yi

CHINA ON THE SUCCESSION OF PU YI, 14 NOVEMBER 1908

Country name: Ta Ch'ing Kuo (Great Ch'ing Kingdom)–Chung Kuo (Middle Kingdom)

Eighteen Provinces of China: 1,500,000 sq. miles. 400,000,000 population.

Capital: Peking, 700,000 population.

Regent: Prince Ch'un

President of the Chinese Foreign Office: Prince Ching

British Adviser to Chinese Government: Sir Walter Hillier

Government: Grand Council and eighteen Boards. Colonial Office ran four Dependencies – Mongolia and Turkestan (both through military lieutenant-generals); Manchuria; and Tibet. Dependencies: 2,500,000 sq. miles; 19,000,000 population. Civil government by viceroys and governors. Each province had Intendants with ten prefectures and districts.

British Diplomatic Presence: Minister: Sir John Jordan, with consuls and vice-consuls. Consul-generals at Canton, Chengtu, Hankow, Mukden, Shanghai, Tientsin with Peking, and Yunnan-fu.

British Residents in China: 9,205 (out of 69,852 resident foreigners). 1,416 British firms represented.

INTRODUCTION

EMPIRE OF THE SON OF HEAVEN

The year is 1884. The place, Falcon Hall School, Edinburgh. A ten-year-old boy sits alone in a classroom staring at a picture. It is his daily routine now to steal away as his classmates play noisily in the policies outside the windows to sit and peer intently at the steel engraving on the wall above the mahogany buffet. The picture shows no real artistry, but the boy is intrigued by its content. The legend reads: 'His Imperial Majesty Kuang-hsu, Son of Heaven, Ch'ing Emperor of China, receives the foreign diplomats.' The picture was gifted to the school by the headmaster's friend Peter Alexander, an Edinburgh-born engineer lately returned from the treaty port of Chefoo, in China's Shantung Province.

Only a week before Alexander had enthralled the Falcon Hall boys with tales of his China adventures. None was more spellbound than Reggie Johnston. The picture had stirred emotions that he could not yet understand, but somehow he knew that one day he would go to the land of the Ch'ing emperors. Fate, too, would entwine his life with that of Emperor Kuang-hsu's nephew Pu Yi in a grim dance of violence, betrayal, exile and exotic adventure as rich as any of the tales of Peter Alexander.[1]

When the 24-year-old Reginald Fleming Johnston arrived in China in 1898, the country was entering a new era of reform. It had been ruled by the Ch'ing Dynasty for almost three hundred years. The dynasty had been founded by the Manchus, a Tungusic people from

China at Reginald Fleming Johnston's arrival in 1898, showing the Treaty Ports. The Treaty of Nanking, 29 August 1842, stated that Canton, Amoy, Foochow, Ningpo and Shanghai should be opened for trade. The cession of Hong Kong to Britain was confirmed and it was developed as a colony. Shanghai was the largest British Settlement in China. Weiheiwei was ceded to Britain on 1 July 1898.

Manchuria, who had risen to power in the sixteenth century. Cleverly they utilized the administrative structure of the ruling Ming dynasty, which had dominated China from 1368, to forge their own powerbase.

Invited by General Wu San-kuie to restore order to the corrupt maelstrom that was China following the suicide of the last Ming Emperor Ch'ung-chan, the Manchus first ruled through a Manchu-Chinese dynasty and were slowly assimilated until they were practically indistinguishable from the Chinese. The dynasty's glory days came in the seventeenth century under the enlightened rule of the open-minded Emperor K'ang-hsi, but the dynasty entered a period of decline in the eighteenth century which degenerated into bloody chaos. There was always a strain of weakness in the dynasty's power for large numbers of the people distrusted them for not being purely Chinese.

As the last years of the eighteenth century slipped away, it was evident that the closed, conservative, xenophobic China, totally uninterested in international trade, would soon come into conflict with the blustering, aggrandizing, mercantile Occident. Even though today's Chinese historians start their studies of 'modern China' in 1840 with the Opium War, the roots of the Chinese–Occidental clash actually go back further.[2]

The first Western visitors to China included the envoys of Pope Nicholas IV to the Kublai Khan under the Franciscan John de Montecorvino during the Yuan period (1279–1368), followed by the Jesuit missionaries of the early Ch'ing period (1644–1911). The latter, with a mixture of guile, diplomacy and sycophancy, extracted much from Chinese culture but never succeeded in affecting the political, economic or social structure of China.

The British and Dutch first traded with China through the East India Company and the *Vereenidge Oost-Indische Compagnie* respectively, both founded in 1602 and both backed by political interests. An early British voyager to China was Captain John Weddell (1583–1642), commander of an expedition which set sail during April 1636, to investigate the possibilities of trade with China. Despite Portuguese resistance Weddell reached Canton for his sponsor, the merchant Sir William Courteene (1572–1636), and with the licence of King Charles I Courteene's Mercantile Association was amalgamated with the Honourable East India Company in 1649.

From 1757 the Chinese authorities restricted all foreign trade to the 'thirteen factories' within the city of Canton (modern Guangzhou) on the Pearl River, and did not allow permanent residency. Outside the trading season, early September to late January, foreign merchants had to retire to the Portuguese-held port of Macao to the west of the Canton delta. Further, they were not permitted to bring their wives or any foreign wares into Canton and were restricted to only a narrow shoreline; trade was limited to certain *hongs* (licensed traders) within their monopolistic *Cohong* under the overall control of the *Hu Bu* (Board of Finance) Controller of Customs appointed by the imperial court. The controllers were consistently corrupt, feathering their own nests through extortionate price-fixing. Foreign merchants were not allowed to employ Chinese servants, learn Chinese, or deal directly with native traders.

These restrictions were a constant irritation to the ostensibly free-trade Europeans, and they resulted in George Macartney's mission to China in 1793. Macartney, 1st Earl Macartney (1737–1806), travelled as King George III's Ambassador Extraordinary and Plenipotentiary, and arrived off Canton on 19 June 1793, proceeding north to Tientsin (modern Tianjin) and then overland to Peking. His brief was to amass information on China, negotiate for a freer trade policy, open up diplomatic relations and persuade the Chinese to cede territory to Britain near to the main trading areas.

In reality the Chinese were not willing to agree to any such proposals nor were they interested in the European concept of free trade; neither were they impressed with the gifts Macartney had brought. Macartney's outright refusal to *kowtow* – the 'three kneelings and nine prostrations' – as he approached the most puissant of the Manchu warrior-sovereigns Emperor Ch'ien-lung, *T'ien-tzu* (Son of

Heaven) at the imperial summer retreat of Jehol outside the Great Wall, further soured the atmosphere.

During 1816 William Pitt, Earl Amherst (1773–1857) and former Governor of India, also refused to *kowtow* on a later mission bent on the same goals as Macartney's, and because of this and other misunderstandings he was refused an audience with Emperor Chia-ch'ing. The Chinese continued to insist that European envoys should observe the grovelling court protocol, as observed by neighbouring states' envoys, and European recalcitrance on this point produced stalemate.

Throughout the nineteenth century the West pressurized China to open her doors, sometimes with the threat of gunboats. And in the end the Chinese were forced to concede, opening up the whole of their country to foreign traders with their missionary camp followers who were later to be the butt of Reginald Fleming Johnston's writings.

In the early days of trade, dominated by the British, a 'triangular trade' was established. British textiles were exported to India; Indian cotton was shipped on to China, and from China to Britain came silk, porcelain and tea. Alas, the Chinese had scant interest in Indian cotton, so silver had to be used to make up the trade deficit. Such a drain on silver supplies demanded that a new commodity had to be found. Thus illegal cargoes of Bengal-grown opium were shipped to China.

The East India Company had been trading in opium since the 1780s and had prospered from the increase in demand in 1819 when the price of the drug had been lowered. Before the British began to ship vast quantities of opium to China the population as a whole was not particularly addicted to the narcotic. It had been used for a long time as a painkiller, but now it became a national addiction as a 'recreational drug'. To distort the economic balance further, the tea plantations that the British had set up in India undermined the demand for China tea, and the silver which had once made up the British–China trade deficit was reversed as Chinese silver flooded into Britain to pay for the opium.

In 1834 the East India Company's trade monopoly came to an end and the British Government appointed a Superintendent of Trade to control foreign commerce and merchants at Canton. As relations with China deteriorated, Superintendent William John Napier, 8th Baron Napier (1786–1834), became unable to satisfy trade negotiations and his successors, appointed in rapid succession, also failed. By 1836 legislation on the legal use of opium and measures to counter the smuggling of the substance were mooted by the Chinese officials, but the legislation was rejected by Emperor Tao-kuang who wished to eradicate entirely the use of opium.

The administrator chosen to destroy the opium trade was Governor Lin Tse-hsu (1785–1850), of Hupei and Hunan provinces, who had already taken steps to eradicate opium addiction in his dual fiefdoms. Lin immediately enacted a severe anti-opium programme. The British Superintendent of Trade, Captain (Sir) Charles Elliot (1801–75), ordered British traders to surrender all their opium to him when he and the traders were put under 'factory compound arrest' by Lin. Elliot then handed over all the opium to Lin who destroyed more than twenty thousand chests of the narcotic.

The whole British community was then allowed to leave Canton on 24 May 1839, and Lin sent a stiff letter to Queen Victoria questioning the morality of the British opium trade. Alas, Her Majesty's Government in London remained unmoved by Lin's threat to sever supplies to Britain of the laxative rhubarb. Prompted largely by commercial and political pressure from almost three hundred companies in London, Manchester and Liverpool, all connected with the China trade, the Liberal Foreign Office Minister Henry John Temple, 3rd Viscount Palmerston (1784–1865), resorted to force and sent gunboats to China.

In due course a 4,000-strong British expeditionary force under Admiral (Sir) George Elliot (1784–1863) arrived off China; their tasks were to secure compensation for the surrender of the opium, confirm future free trade at Canton and demand satisfaction for the illegal detention of British officials. A blockade of the Chinese coast was set in place to 'encourage' China to play a role in the negotiations. The scene was set for a three-phase Opium War.

During phase one, June 1840 to January 1841, the British seized Chusan (south of Shanghai), blockaded ports from Ningpo to the mouth of the Yangtze Kiang, and advanced to Pei-ho near Tientsin, thus threatening Peking. In response, an alarmed Emperor Tao-kuang sacked Tin Tse-shu and assured the British, through Governor-General Ch'i-shan of Tientsin, that a settlement could be reached. The British withdrew south. Vacillation on the part of the Chinese caused Captain Elliot, now following up British interests, to attack the Ch'uan-pi forts, forcing Ch'i-shan to sign the Ch'uan-pi Convention indemnifying Hong Kong to the British and re-opening the Canton trade. Emperor Tao-kuang promptly rejected Ch'i-shan's draft and sacked him. Back in Britain, Palmerston likewise rejected the draft because of the 'woolliness' of the British demands for Hong Kong, and Captain Elliot was replaced by Sir Henry Pottinger (1789–1856).

When Pottinger arrived in August 1841 the Opium War had passed through its second phase – the successful British siege of Canton. Pottinger extended British military dominance in the third phase along the Chinese coast, occupying Shanghai by the spring of 1842. By cutting the Grand Canal he threatened Nanking. The Chinese realized that they had been outgunned and outmanoeuvred. In the Treaty of Nanking, signed on 29 August 1842, the international status of China was transformed; Hong Kong, reparation and residency rights were ceded to the British, along with the opening of China's five Treaty Ports: Canton, Amoy island, Foochow on the Min River, Ningpo on the southern side of the Yangtze delta, and Shanghai. This treaty, and subsequent agreements with France and the USA, promoted the development of international settlements in China.[3] In 1854 Sir John Bowring (1792–1872), the former British Consul at Canton, was appointed to the post of Minister Plenipotentiary to the Court at Peking.

During the period of thirty years from 1840 China was in turmoil, with many internal rebellions fomented by the opportunistic outlaws and agitators. The most important was the Taiping Rebellion of 1856–64, the roots of which lay in peasant hardships through droughts, severe floods and famine.[4] The Taiping agitators, led by Hung Hsiu-ch'uan, caused trouble for the neutral British consuls who were forced in some cases to negotiate with them in order to sustain their trade flow. Pursuing their rebellion against the weakening Ch'ing dynasty, the *Taiping* ('Supreme Peace') captured Nanking where they established their main government, and for a decade the tides of conflict ebbed and flowed. Britain was eventually forced to defend her Shanghai possessions and Charles George Gordon (1833–85) of the Royal Engineers fought thirty-three actions against the Taipings, earning himself the nickname 'Chinese Gordon'.

The various rebellions formed a dangerous backdrop to international expansion in China and the rise of a new business class, as numbers of Chinese emigrated to the goldfields of California and Australia. While dealing with internal rebellion, the ruling group in China had also to cope with foreign pressure to exact the treaty rights.

By the 1850s Britain had three Consular Services which were the backbone of the colonial service in which Reginald Fleming Johnston played a prominent part. The General Service, reformed in 1825, was at large in most of the civilized world, working for the protection of trade. As diplomat Frank Ashton-Gwatkin (1889–1976) pointed out, it was not held in particular high regard.[5] The Levant Service, based on the old Levant Company, covered the relevant areas of the Near and Middle East and was designated as a separate service in 1877. The Levant Service officers had wider political and judicial remits than those of the General Service.[6]

The China Consular Service had been formed in 1858 with functions similar to the Levant Service. Recruits had to speak Chinese (a necessity for promotion) and were well paid, although previously diplomats were expected to have private means.[7] The structure of the colonial service was to survive until the Second World War. Recruits came from three main sources: military or commercial backgrounds; university campuses; and others of 'good education'. Unlike their possessions in India, the British did not rule their China enclaves through colonial government (except Hong Kong). In the treaty ports they developed a system of local government through municipal councils. These depended upon the mores of *extraterritoriality* which exempted Britons from local (Chinese) laws. This privilege had been won via the Treaty of Nanking and the Convention of Chefoo of 1876.

When Reginald Fleming Johnston arrived in China the British Foreign Service was headed by Sir Claude Maxwell Macdonald (1852–1915) as British Minister at Peking. Before transferring to Tokyo, Macdonald would organize the defence of the legations during the Boxer Rising of 1900. Macdonald was succeeded by the distinguished sinologist and Japanologist Sir Ernest Mason Satow (1843–1929). By 1898 Britain had consulates at Tientsin, Peking, Canton, Shanghai and Newchwang, with a Chief Justice of the Supreme Court for China and Korea at Shanghai. Established in 1865, this court administered complete civil and criminal law and Admiralty jurisdiction over British subjects in China and Korea.[8] In London the emperor was represented by Sir Chichen Lo Feng-hui from his embassy in Portland Place.

The Second Opium War, also known as the 'Arrow War', broke out in 1856 when the Chinese refused to apologize for an insult to the British flag aboard the lorcha *Arrow*, a Chinese-owned vessel.[9] When the *Arrow* entered the Pearl River at Canton on the morning of 8 October a Chinese patrol boarded her to search for pirates. Arrests were made and the British flag was lowered. The British Consul at Canton, Sir Harry Smith Parkes (1828–85), protested to Governor Yeh Ming-ch'en and demanded the return of the arrested Chinese seamen with an apology. When the latter was refused the minor issue flared into war.

The French supported the British, as the French missionary Abbé Chapdelaine had been murdered, and the Chinese were once more defeated. In June 1858 the British and French secured more new treaty ports, mostly along the Yangtze, indemnity, freedom of movement for foreigners in China, and the placing of resident foreign ministers at Peking, within the Treaty of Tientsin. The Chinese did not fully cooperate with the treaty negotiations until James Bruce, 8th Earl of Elgin (1811–63), stormed Canton, along with the French diplomat Baron Gros, in order to extract greater concessions at the final peace settlements within the Convention of Peking of 1860.

On 21 February 1875 Augustus Raymond Margary (b. 1846), a British consular interpreter and vice-consul, was murdered at Monwein on the China–Burma frontier. The British Government held the Chinese responsible and called for the arrest and trial of the acting Governor-general of Yunnan and Kweichow. After a British threat to suspend diplomatic relations, the case was settled by the Convention of Chefoo of 1876 which gave the bereaved family a cash indemnity and included trade privileges. The events led to the first Chinese resident legation abroad.

From 1860 to 1895 China went through a dynastic revival under the emperors T'ung-chih and Kuang-hsu, along with a period of 'self-strengthening' through Western learning, scientific and technological knowledge, military strategy and diplomacy. Meanwhile foreign powers pursued a policy of cooperation with the Chinese authorities to consolidate the treaty concessions they had squeezed out of China. The 'self-strengthening' policy was to be tested when China decided to resist the French aspirations in Annam (modern Vietnam), the British in Burma and the Japanese in Manchuria and Korea. In the Franco-Chinese War Annam was lost by China by 1885 as a tributary state and became a French protectorate; in the same year the British made Burma a protectorate, and a dangerous situation was brewing in Korea and Manchuria with Japan ready to pounce.

The Sino-Japanese War (1 August 1894 to 17 April 1895) was a conflict that startled the West. Japan quickly and utterly defeated

China's superior forces and emerged as the dominant East Asian power. On land, the Huai Army of Li Hung-chang was routed at P'yongyang on 16 September 1894, and the next day the old and slow vessels of the Peiyang Fleet were crushed at the naval battle of the Yalu River. By 21 November the naval ports, bases and shipyards of Port Arthur and Dairen had fallen to the Imperial Japanese Navy. The Chinese fleet was destroyed at Weiheiwei on 12 February 1895.

A peace settlement was forced through by the Treaty of Shimonoseki of 17 April. In the main this provided for the independence of Korea, but it also opened the door to Japanese incursion, a cash indemnity for Japan and the ceding to Japan of Formosa (Taiwan), the Pescadores and the Liatoung peninsula. Importantly, China became an object for Japanese exploitation in terms of territorial control and colonization, and the seeds of national humiliation were sown that were to be reaped as internal rebellion.[10] Further, the conflict marked modern Japan's future role in international power politics, which would end in the Second World War, and would directly involve Reginald Fleming Johnston and his imperial pupil.

The history of the Far East thus began a new era. At sea Japan began to rival the Royal Navy while on land the might of Czarist Russia was challenged by the Imperial Japanese Army. At home China was gripped in the dual vortices of foreign pressure and popular unrest as China's territories fragmented and passed into the control of Germany, Russia, Britain and France.

All these factors encouraged demands for reform in China and the ill-fated reform movement was instigated in 1898; the prime mover was the Confucian scholar K'ang Yu-wei (1858–1927), who was impressed by the administration of the British-dominated cities. The failure of the Hundred Days Reform Movement when K'ang Yu-wei fled the arrest orders of the Grand Empress Dowager Tzu Hsi was to precipitate the Boxer movement and the Revolutionary Republican Movement. Into this maelstrom would step the 24-year-old Reginald Fleming Johnston.

The Chinese Treaty Ports in which they had won concessions were regarded by the British as an extension of their Empire. By 1898 they had two Chinese colonies, one at Weiheiwei, with which Reginald Fleming Johnston was to be greatly concerned, and the other in Hong Kong, and the largest British settlement was at Shanghai. Most of the British settlers were missionaries or businessmen: the first bent on changing the culture, the second hoping to win for their companies the undoubted profits that were to be had and to enjoy the 'life of ease'. Although they were Johnston's compatriots he grew to loathe both types, but particularly the missionaries. By the time Johnston went to Hong Kong the British, like all other foreigners living in the concession areas, enjoyed an almost diplomatic privilege of freedom from arrest or prosecution in a Chinese court. All the enclaves in China, whether Japanese, German, French, Russian or British, were microcosms of their native lands.

Reginald Fleming Johnston was following in the footsteps of famous men in the Chinese Consular and Colonial Services: people like Alcock, Hart and Giles. Sir Rutherford Alcock (1809–97) had been consul at Foochow and Shanghai, and during 1865–71 was Minister Plenipotentiary at Peking. As a mentor to young 'cadets' from Britain, Alcock taught that a firm line should be taken with orientals. He noted that 'a salutary dread of the immediate consequences of violence offered to British subjects . . . seems to be the best and only protection in this country for Englishmen'.[11] Alcock's ability to get things done was the result of two attributes that Johnston also found relevant, namely patience and persistence. Like Johnston, Alcock did not approve of the often unscrupulous behaviour of British businessmen and adventurers in China. Sir Robert Hart (1835–1911), Inspector-General of the Chinese Imperial Maritime Customs, developed his brief into an international force of great advantage to Britain. Dr Herbert Alan Giles (1845–1935) served in the China Consular Service during 1867–93 and became Professor of Chinese at Cambridge. He, like Johnston, produced writings that promoted an intelligent understanding of Chinese culture.

Yet no British expatriate of the age was ever to study China to the extent and in the detail undertaken by Reginald Fleming Johnston, who soaked himself in Chinese culture and became a neo-Confucian. Johnston saw China as his spiritual home and was given unique privileges of observing the nation, its people and its culture. His admittance to the closed imperial court was an opportunity never before given to a Westerner and his life there and its consequences weave a story rich in adventure and intrigue.

CHAPTER 1

EARLY LIFE: EDINBURGH TO HONG KONG

Morningside – the sunny 'morning side' – on the southern slopes of Edinburgh originated as a secluded hamlet of thatched cottages serving an agricultural community. Its 'mild salubrious air'[1] made it a popular summer retreat from the foetid streets of the workaday city, while the introduction of the Edinburgh Suburban and South Side Junction Railway in 1885 made it a throbbing adjunct to the developing metropolis.[2]

To the right, off Morningside Road, on the line of the old route south from Edinburgh's Tollcross district to the Lanarkshire country town of Biggar, where Prime Minister William Gladstone's ancestors lived, the biblically named Canaan Lane and Jordan Lane form two sides of a rectangular area that was to develop in the nineteenth century as a quiet haven of villas and mansions known locally as Goshen. Along a small lane lay the early nineteenth-century, two-storey, three-bay sandstone Goshen Bank House.[3] For a short while from 1868 Henry Kingsley (1830–76), editor of the *Edinburgh Daily Review*, and the brother of Charles Kingsley (1819–75) the author of *The Water Babies*, lived at Goshen Bank House, but its most famous inhabitant locally was to be born here less than a decade later.[4] On 13 October 1874 was born Reginald Fleming Johnston, the eldest of the three children of Robert Fleming Johnston (1840–1902), Writer to the Signet,[5] and his wife Isabella Anne Catherine Johnston whom he had married on 22 May 1872.[6]

The Johnstons had originated in Dumfriesshire where their ancestors had been members of a powerful clan, famous in Scots song and story. They derived their name from the Barony of Johnston in Annandale and the name occurs in records from the thirteenth century. Mrs Johnston was an Irving, second daughter of the Revd Charles Irving, Church of Ireland Rector of Donoughmore, Co. Donegal, Ireland.[7]

Robert Fleming Johnston was a partner, with his superior and mentor John Richardson, in the law firm of Richardson & Johnston, whose wherewithal had been founded on the Midlothian properties and reputation of his father John Smith Johnston, who had practised in Scotland's Supreme Court and undertook important litigation work in Forfarshire.[8] Until his death on 12 July 1902 Robert had been associated with the firm of J. & R.A. Robertson, who remained the family lawyers until the death of Reginald Fleming Johnston.[9]

Reginald Fleming Johnston's siblings, Constance Margaretta Fleming Johnston (b. Goshen Bank, 5 May 1873) – dubbed 'Noney' – and Charles Edward Fleming Johnston (b. Goshen Bank, 16 November 1876) are hardly relevant to his story. Edward went to America and was associated with the Emma Willard Conservatory of Music at Troy in New York. He was married and sired a daughter Emily, while Noney married twice and bore a daughter Rosemary. Correspondence shows that the three siblings did not get along very well, and latterly Reggie refused to write to them or even meet them.[10] Noney went on to own dog kennels, breeding cairn terriers for shows, and eked out a meagre living with some journalism.

* * *

During his very early years, before his mother's extravagance and his father's business misfortunes took their toll, Reginald Fleming Johnston's family lived comfortably in Morningside's developing middle class area. As befitted the son of an Edinburgh lawyer, young

Reggie was destined for a professional career within his father's office. At the time Robert Johnston believed that the best education was to be obtained through the standards required by the Civil Service.

On his matriculation application for the University of Oxford,[11] Reginald Fleming Johnston noted that he had been educated by 'private tuition' and at two private elementary schools. The first of these was Strathmore House School, 30 Queen Street, Southport, Merseyside. This school was then comparatively new, having been founded some time between 1873 and 1875, and was run by one Francis Rigg MA, who had a good reputation as a 'crammer tutor' for Civil Service examinations.[12] Young Reggie stayed here for a year and a half.

From Strathmore House he went to Falcon Hall School which lay a short distance from Goshen towards the city. The buildings of the now vanished school were commissioned in 1815 by Alexander Falconer, who emphasized his name by having stone falcons atop the main gate of his residence by Morningside Road. Falconer had served in the Indian Civil Service and was a former Secretary to the Governor of Madras.[13]

In 1889 a high-class boarding school for boys was opened at Falcon Hall to prepare pupils for entry into the Indian Civil Service, the Army (Sandhurst) and the Royal Navy (Woolwich). The school was the first in Scotland to prepare pupils for these specific entrance examinations. Education at Falcon Hall was under the direction of retired Army tutor Dr Devey Fearon Ranking, who had moved his own school, founded in 1885, from Rockville House, 3 Napier Road, Merchiston, Edinburgh, to this site.[14]

In a rare personal revelation, Reginald Fleming Johnston noted in a letter to his lawyer Robert Augustus Robertson that he left Falcon Hall in 1890.[15] He describes how he went into his father's law office and mentions his extreme dislike of the office routines. In his spare time he pursued a programme of self-education and a year or two later persuaded his father to allow him to work half-days at the office and spend the rest of the time at private tuition. His tutor was the 25-year-old

David Playfair Heatley, then engaged in historical research in the University of Edinburgh.[16] Heatley encouraged Johnston to attend classes at the university and he matriculated during the 1892/93 Session. In the 1894/95 Session Johnston shared the Gray Essay Prize of £20 with Francis Dewar Hill from Ratho.[17]

Heatley was impressed enough with Johnston's potential to encourage him to apply for a history scholarship at Magdalen College, Oxford. This Johnston did and was successful, being granted the sum of £50 per annum for the years 1894–98; he appeared in Oxford as an Exhibitioner.[18] During this time Johnston records that he lived frugally, funded by his father to the sum of £150 per annum.[19]

From 1894 to 1896 Johnston lived in the same set of rooms in the New Building and from 1896 until 1898 within the older buildings of Magdalen College. Because of his reticence in personal matters, little is known about Johnston's college days, and whether he took part in society or club life to any great extent. Magdalen, with its College Tower of 1492–1507, greatly appealed to Johnston's sense of history and still had the ambience enjoyed by Oscar Wilde and his lover Lord Alfred Douglas; its president, Sir Thomas Herbert Warren (1853–1930), presided over a distinguished staff of dons and an ever-increasing number of undergraduates.

In another rare example of self-revelation, in a letter to Sir James Lockhart he reminisces about Magdalen and dwells on his love of the college chapel.[20] As he sat in the graduate stalls robed in an MA gown he recalled on a December day in 1913 listening to a passage from Robert Schumann's *Requiem*. He communed, he said, with the ghosts of his youth, allowing his usually buttoned-up emotions to be imbued with both pain and pleasure. Magdalen was one of the two places in the world he loved the most and he visited whenever he could.

Reginald Fleming Johnston had three close friends at Oxford:[21] Sir Cecil Clementi (1875–1947), the future governor of Hong Kong (1925–30); F. Paul Armitage (1875–1953), Director of Education for the City of Leicester (1919–40); and Dr Thomas Loveday

(1875–1966), Vice-Chancellor of the University of Bristol (1922–26), where Johnston would be a future visiting lecturer.[22] In his circle of fellow-undergraduates were Sir Harold Morris (1876–1967), lawyer and MP, Major Thomas Broke (1875–1954), and Sir Arthur Page (1876–1958), Chief Justice of Burma (1930–31). Johnston was to be a lifelong correspondent with Clementi, Armitage and Loveday.

Johnston graduated BA(Oxon) with a 2nd Class degree in Modern History on 20 October 1898 and received an honourable mention for the Stanhope Essay Prize in the same year.[23] On coming down from Oxford Johnston entered himself for the Indian Civil Service examination.[24] In those days applicants who gained top marks in this examination were offered positions in the Home Civil Service departments, while those who received the lowest grades were offered the Levant Civil Service or 'Eastern cadetships'. Johnston's obituary in *The Times*[25] refers to a 'technical disqualification' in his application which ruled out employment in the Indian Empire, and he was offered a cadetship in Hong Kong. He accepted the offer.

* * *

The island of Hong Kong presented the Victorian traveller with a seductive panorama of the picturesque Orient. Its very name was an allurement and always defied an acceptable translation, be it 'Perfumed Harbour' or 'Sweet-scented Bay'. As Assistant Colonial Secretary Reginald Fleming Johnston was now a member of the British Crown Colony Staff who endeavoured to bring cohesion and regularity to a population and area that was fluid and inchoate.

Hong Kong has no history relevant to this story before its occupation by the British. The island was first occupied by the Royal Navy on 26 January 1841 during the Opium War, but it was not legally ceded to the Crown until the Treaty of Nanking in August 1842. The Foreign Secretary of the day, Henry John Temple, 3rd Viscount Palmerston (1784–1865), dismissed Hong Kong as 'a barren island with hardly a house upon it', and Queen Victoria considered it something of a joke.[26] In April 1841 she wrote to her uncle Leopold I, King of the Belgians (1790–1865): 'Albert is so much amused at my having got the island of Hong Kong, and we think Victoria [the queen's eldest child, Vicky (1840–1901)] ought to be called Princess of Hong Kong in addition to Princess Royal.'[27]

From the first days of British rule through its first Governor, Sir Henry Pottinger (1789–1856), Hong Kong was administered as a 'unique case'. An annexed part of the vast, amorphous, arcane China, it was a centre of the opium trade and it attracted both wealthy merchants and the riff-raff of the China seas. The firm Jardine, Matheson & Co., founded by Dr William Jardine in the 1830s, was transferred to Hong Kong which developed as a commercial centre.[28]

When Reginald Fleming Johnston first disembarked at Hong Kong, after the usual thirty-one days of sea passage, he entered a world as different from his native Scotland as would be the moon.

China was a vast, rambling, semi-feudal, semi-colonial country, and one diplomat described Hong Kong as 'the impudent British pimple on the backside of China'. By a convention signed on 9 June 1898, China granted Britain a lease for ninety-nine years on Lan-tau island (due west of Hong Kong island). Kowloon peninsula (facing Hong Kong) had been leased to Sir Harry Parkes by the Governor-General, Liang Kuang, and was ceded to the British by the Convention of Peking on 24 October 1860. This gave Hong Kong an area of 293 square miles, with a further 376 square miles of concessions; in 1898 the total population was 259,312. Tea, coffee and silk were traded out of the capital Victoria – originally Queen's Town – alongside the more sinister opium trade. When Johnston arrived, the opium trade was worth some £5 million and licences for the 'divans' (smoking-halls) contributed some two million Hong Kong dollars to the colony's local government purse.

The Crown Colony to which Reginald Fleming Johnston was introduced had a colonial structure based on a government and council of eight under a governor. From 25 November 1898 this post was filled by Limerick-born Irishman Sir Henry Arthur Blake (1840–1918), formerly Captain-General and General-in-Chief of Jamaica. Whitehall had briefed Hong Kong's first Governor, Sir Henry Pottinger, that the gubernatorial duty was threefold: to foster good relations with the Emperor's court at Peking; to maintain and protect the interests of British citizens in the Chinese Treaty Ports; and – almost as an afterthought – to seek to construct a constitutional framework to govern and keep order over swarms of Occidental and Oriental immigrants to the south-east China sea region. Blake took up this brief and through a legislative council the British were governed under British law, while the Chinese were subject to Chinese law and traditions, except if they conflicted with what Whitehall jargon defined as 'those immutable principles of morality which Christians must regard as binding on themselves at all times and in all places'.[29]

From the beginning the British concessions called the New Territories, north of Hong Kong island, were a source of trouble. The region had been populated for decades by Chinese landlords and peasants, and consisted largely of old walled villages and temples. In some ways the emperor's viceroys at Canton were pleased to get shot of this area, as it was a source of fierce village feuds. United in their resentment for the arrival of the British, the peoples hereabouts had regular scuffles with the authorities. The British military occupation was completed by April 1898 and one of Johnston's first reports concerned Hong Kong's New Territories problems. In short, the long border with China had to be controlled, complex systems of customs dues had to be negotiated, land revenue had to be collected and new roads and a new railway had to be planned and built, linking Kowloon and Canton.

By the time Reginald Fleming Johnston arrived at Victoria on Christmas Day 1898, it had developed from a huddle of shacks, tents, go-downs and palm-leafed huts into a solid, prosperous, tropical city, spilling out along Hong Kong island's northern shore and clambering up the steep terraces of the slopes of Victoria Peak. (The Peak could be viewed in comfort, after the opening of the Peak tramway in 1897, removing the need for a long, strenuous climb.) Victoria's streets hummed with the commercial business of the day, while soldiers and sailors dodged sedan-chairs and scarlet-curtained palanquins to mingle with mandarins in pigtails, resplendent in the gold-threaded garments and jade-button hats of their rank. Ever noisy, the byways echoed to the shouts of the rickshaw boys and the squabbling chatter of the sampan girls along the waterfront.

Johnston soon encountered the sophisticated social life of European Hong Kong, which had become more self-conscious after the first visit by a member of Queen Victoria's family. Her grandson Prince Henry of Prussia (1862–1929) – the second son of Princess Victoria and Frederick III, the German Emperor and King of Prussia – stayed at Government House and Hong Kong society jostled for invitations to meet him at the Queen's Birthday Dinner on 26 May and at a State lunch-party given by the Governor Sir John Pope-Hennessy (1834–91).

In 1898 Hong Kong's social life was colourful and confident. This was the high noon of Empire: people were making more money than ever before and Hong Kong society was lavish enough to match that of Victorian – and soon Edwardian – London. The activities on the island revolved around a number of institutions. The Royal Navy dockyards and the Hong Kong garrison at Wellington Barracks and North Barracks each had their own 'circles', and from time to time their commanding officers were at odds, either with one another over alleged infringements of privileges, or with the governor because of his policies.

During Johnston's time, the ratio of servicemen to civilians remained high and their centre was the Hong Kong Club of 1846. There were also Roman Catholic and Anglican communities and the interconnecting social circles of missionary education and hospital charities. Shooting and fishing parties were popular for the men while the women took tea and sported the very latest fashions from London, or played chaperoned tennis with the young subalterns.

The British tended to be cliquish when it came to the ethnic Chinese, although by and large the leading Chinese were also 'clannish' and exclusive, playing very little role in the British way of life and preferring their children, for instance, to be educated outside Hong Kong at Canton, rather than in the English schools on the island. The Chinese leaders took little part in politics and could be difficult, stirring up strikes among the house boys, maids and clerks who worked for the British if Foreign Office legislation displeased them. The British tended to be transient, with little interest in Chinese culture and beliefs.[30]

Reginald Fleming Johnston was the exact opposite of the typical uncaring British expatriate, being interested more in Chinese than British company; although he was by nature reclusive he came alive in stimulating company, especially with compatriots who showed an interest in his growing devotion to oriental studies.

Charles Leonard Moore (1874–1947) remembered Johnston in his early 'cadet' days:

> I met Reg soon after he arrived in Hong Kong in those heady days when HMG [Her Majesty's Government] took over the ceded territories, and worked with him for a while before I joined the Japan Service [extra consular posts were created because of Japan's expanding concessions in the Far East]. He was one of the jolliest 'cadets' I ever met (when it suited him) and was a very magpie in collecting snippets about Chinese history and cultural traditions. As I look back [the entry was written in retrospect as an obituary note on Johnston's death in 1938] I recognize that few Europeans ever had the expanse or depth of knowledge about China than he. From a humble academic background Reg emerged from Magdalen to become a scholar, traveller and writer, who someone said made him like 'Lawrence of Arabia'. He was a good colleague to work with

> and I know that Blake [Sir Henry Blake, Governor of Hong Kong, 1898–1903] and Lockhart [Sir James Lockhart, Commissioner at Weiheiwei] thought highly of him. Kitty [Moore's wife, Catherine Margaret Johnston] and I always found him a stimulating companion (although he could be cold and reserved to those who bored him), and his schoolboy laughter and enthusiasm brightened many a day. Kitty says he would have made a good father as he had a naturalness with children, and the Chinese children in the villages around Cherry Glen [Johnston's Chinese home in the Western Hills] flocked round him whenever he appeared on one of his 'temple visits'. Yet, I have to admit he was what the modern fashionable psychologists would call a 'complex man'; one day he was the hermit scholar, the next the driving force behind a Civil Service directive. For Kitty and me he always remained a generous companion and a true friend.[31]

In 1898 Reginald Fleming Johnston embarked on his lifelong study of the Chinese people, their traditions and annals, and was a witness to some of the most momentous occasions in the history of the Far East. In Hong Kong began the chain of events that would bring him international recognition.

CHAPTER 2

The Young Cadet: Boxers, Bandits and Bible-Thumpers

The pattern of Reginald Fleming Johnston's working life before he was posted to Weiheiwei in 1904 was clear. For five years, from 1899, he was acting clerk to the Administrative Councils in Hong Kong and Assistant Colonial Secretary within the Crown Colony. From 1900 to 1902 he was private secretary to Governor Sir Henry Blake. In the year that Johnston arrived in Hong Kong, important developments were taking place in China proper. At a reception at Government House, he met one of the key figures in these events, the radical reformer K'ang Yu-wei. A respected Confucian scholar, K'ang had been impressed by the British administration of their concessions at Shanghai and Hong Kong and in 1883 gave up his civil service career to devote his efforts to studying the West and writing about proposed reforms for archaic China.

In a series of 'memorials' – suggestions of policy changes – K'ang and others endeavoured to persuade Emperor Kuang-hsu to adopt a constitutional mode of monarchy, to modernize the examination system and administration structure of China and to establish the equivalent of a European-style national assembly or parliament. The proposals were anathema to the Empress Dowager Tzu Hsi, who feared that they would undermine her own power. However, in 1898 they were to spawn what was to become known as the Hundred Days Reform.

During September of this year, too, the Empress Dowager took on once more a dominant role in the government of China and ordered the arrest of the 'dangerous' K'ang Yu-wei. Hence his appearance as a refugee in Hong Kong, where he sought and received from the British police protection against possible assassination while en route to Singapore. The failure of K'ang Yu-wei's reform movement led to an escalation of discontent in China that would lead to all-out republican revolution; the first steps of the process were to be recorded by Johnston in official memos.

From his early days in Hong Kong Reginald Fleming Johnston absorbed as many aspects of Chinese life as he could and his meeting with K'ang Yu-wei increased his interest in Confucianism. Born in the sixth century BC, Confucius remains the most prominent and most revered of all the traditional Chinese philosophers. Born K'ung-fu-tzu in the State of Lu (modern Shantung) to a minor aristocratic family, he left a series of lowly official posts to wander through China in search of a position suitable to his capabilities. His scholarly works preached that government administration should be based on ethics rather than pragmatic politics. His ideal man was the *chun-tzu* (gentleman) who was in command of five cardinal virtues: altruism, conscientiousness, humanity, uprightness and righteousness, all culturally oiled by an understanding of etiquette. Confucius emphasized that *jen* (humanity or goodness) should be the founding principle of human intercourse. Johnston was to study Confucius throughout his life, making it the key factor of his devotion 'to the study of the language, history and civilization of the Shantung province'.[1]

The Chinese rulers, from the time of the Ming emperors (1368–1644), considered the Chinese system of government to be the finest in the world since it was based on the series of Confucian moral laws, which most Westerners first encountered in his *Analects*. His principles determined the relationship between rulers and ruled, wherein rulers had a moral duty to behave responsibly and generously towards those ruled. Thus social differences of rank were divinely ordained. The respect for knowledge and intellect inculcated by Confucius in his disciples led to the Chinese meritocracy in government whereby mandarins (scholars) were in charge of provinces and the top echelons of the imperial administration were open only to an élite who had proved themselves in difficult examinations. Johnston found that what made Chinese government unique was that this intellectual élite was in loyal and unquestioning service to the imperial dynasty that espoused and magnified a medieval perspective on the world. This insularity of mind ran in parallel with a penchant for personal and state secrecy that encouraged a passion for intrigue and a frame of mind which even called the environs of the emperor the Forbidden City.

That Confucianism was the key to Johnston's personality was spelled out by his early biographical analyst Roger Soame Jenyns, of the Oriental Antiquities and Ethnography Department of the British Museum:

> This is the secret to an understanding of Johnston's character for . . . he became to all intents and purposes a Confucianist. He could write sympathetically of Buddhism and Taoism although he felt that either of these could be extinguished without loss, but Confucianism . . . could not be annihilated without irreparable harm to the seal and body politic of China.[2]

On 30 December 1898 Johnston informed the Hong Kong Administrative Council that cables had been received from Peking reporting the murder of an English Christian missionary by members of a secret society called *I Ho Ch'uan* (Society of the Righteous and Harmonious Fists), dubbed the Boxer Movement by the occidentals in China.[3] Two days later Johnston circulated to council members the ambiguous Imperial Edict criticizing the assassination, which was one of a growing number of such attacks on the *yang kuai tzu* (foreign devils) and Christians by secret societies. Behind the violence lay decades of Chinese disaffection that was to spill out on to the world stage.[4]

Britain, France, Germany, Italy, Russia and Japan had been dividing China for years. Mining and railroad projects had extracted huge concessions from China; the Chinese economy was slowly coming under the control of international cadres and some two thousand Christian missionaries had flooded into the foreign-appropriated ports. What annoyed the Chinese was that the Westerners were living in luxury at their expense, depressing China's economy, while the missionaries, their families and hangers-on were flouting Chinese laws through extraterritoriality.

As the century came to a close several secret societies were formed in China in an effort to thwart European and Christian expansion. The Boxers, in their central stronghold of the economically depressed Shantung area, where the British occupied Weiheiwei and the Germans the Kiaochou peninsula, were dedicated to the destruction of the Christian religion in China; they sought the murder of foreign and Chinese Christians, and worked for the removal of foreign influence in administration and commerce. In reality, as a military force the Boxers were useless, but these largely uneducated, naive yet headstrong fighters, their hair tied up in red bandanas and wearing blood-red girdles, wreaked a destructive havoc.

In Peking the ruling Manchu dynasty was dominated by the Empress Dowager Tzu Hsi, with her nephew the Emperor Kuang-hsu as a figurehead. Tzu Hsi and her advisers encouraged the Boxers, for the secret society was doing precisely what the Imperial Government could not do – attacking the *yang kuai tzu* in a conflict that for a few months diverted British attention away from the horrors of the South African War. The Boxer uprising started along the Shantung–Chihli borderland, where the Northern China mountains were high and the imperial law and order was far away.

In late January 1900 the continual attacks and harassment of foreigners – and any Chinese people who gave them succour or had been converted to Christianity – resulted in formal notes being delivered by British diplomats, and other foreign embassies in Peking, to the Imperial

Government in protest at the outrages. The foreign legations began to strengthen their defences and British troops were moved north from Hong Kong. The Imperial Government did nothing to stop the attacks and by May the Boxers were riding high on a wave of resentment against foreigners and they attacked villages and slaughtered Chinese Christians. In Shansi Province alone some two thousand Chinese Christians and sixty foreign missionaries were executed, forty of them by the direct orders of the Manchu pro-Boxer provincial governor Yu-hsien. Christians now began flocking to areas of safety in Treaty Ports and diplomatic compounds. As the Boxers swept through the country, disrupting trade, cutting communications and harassing foreigners, the Imperial Court officials hissed through their teeth at audiences the ambiguous platitudes of regret to indignant diplomats.

During June, as a part of the Chinese uprisings against foreigners, the governor of Manchuria attacked the Russians across the Amur River. For a long time the Russians had cast covetous glances at the region and now they attacked in retaliation. On 6 June the Boxers severed all rail links between Peking and the garrison town of Tientsin, the main port for Peking, where the *Da Yunhe* (Grand Canal) joins the Hai River. Three days later they destroyed Peking racecourse, a symbol of Western social life and privilege. Ambassadors and ministers within the diplomatic compounds at Peking, known collectively as the Foreign Legations, refused to evacuate their women and children but requested Admiral Sir Edward Hobart Seymour (1840–1929), the Commander-in-Chief China Station and the senior ranking officer among the foreign services in China, to bring up to Peking reinforcements in the shape of seventeen warships then moored at their base in Taku Bay, Tientsin.

By mid-June 1900 the Foreign Legations were almost marooned by the violence prevailing in the Peking streets. The compounds of the legations covered some 3 acres and housed eleven foreign embassies, each of around sixty people; their numbers now swelled to include some 450 foreigners, 450 naval guards and 300 Chinese Christians.

Their nominal leader was the British minister, Sir Claude Maxwell Macdonald. Boxers continued to rampage through the Peking streets, setting fire to whole quarters of the city. In a show of strength foreign vessels began to bombard the Taku forts and the defences were stormed by the international naval brigade.

On 17 June the Empress Dowager Tzu Hsi requested all foreign diplomats to leave for Tientsin. To everyone in the Foreign Legations it was painfully clear that they were trapped, and the imperious, impatient German minister, Baron Freiherr Klemens von Ketteler, decided to go personally to the Chinese authorities to demand protection for anyone in the legations who wished to go to Tientsin. On his way to the authorities on 20 June he was shot at point-blank range. Nine days before, the Japanese had protested at the murder of the Chancellor of their legation, Akira Sugiyama. These murders convinced the other diplomats that they should stay put.

The Imperial Court, on 1 June, had issued a statement that virtually amounted to a declaration of war on foreigners in China. Its impact was such that the Boxers – now dubbed 'righteous people' by the court circle – increased their attacks on foreigners with greater ferocity and intensity and the slaughter worsened, particularly in Shantung and Manchuria.

By 22 June virtually all the foreign community in Peking had fled to the British compound along with the many Chinese Christians. The Boxers set fire to nearby buildings to try to smoke them out but succeeded only in destroying important Chinese records in the *Hanlin Yuan*, the prestigious library of Chinese scholarship. Russia and Japan now mobilized troops to help contain the Boxer uprising, but only as a part of their long-term plans for China.

As July went by, international forces took Tientsin and on 4 August a huge international force set off to relieve the legations at Peking, which it successfully did on the 14th. On 15 August the Empress Dowager, with some of her family and retainers, fled Peking, taking with them Emperor Kuang-hsu. International troops and resident foreigners embarked on a shameful rampage, looting Chinese treasures, although they were ordered to stay out of the innermost part of the Forbidden City. On 30 September Russian forces took Mukden (Shenyang), virtually completing their occupation of Manchuria which they had invaded in July.

For two months the Allied powers argued among themselves as to what should be done with the China problem and the negotiations for peace. During December 1900 the foreign powers submitted their Twelve Demands:

1. China was to express public regrets for the murder of Baron von Ketteler and erect a monument to his memory;
2. All those identified as responsible for the rebellion were to be punished;
3. Japan was to be recompensed for the murder of Minister Sugiyama;
4. China should produce no more arms;
5. Indemnities should be paid;
6. Foreigners should have the right to keep guards in the legation area;
7. The Taku forts were to be destroyed;
8. Foreigners were to be able to guard their lines of communication to the sea;
9. It would be made a capital offence to belong to an anti-foreign society;
10. New treaties must be negotiated with foreign powers;
11. Cemeteries for foreigners desecrated by the Boxers must be repaired;
12. The Chinese Government must reform the *Tsungli Yamen* (Foreign Ministry).

On 13 February 1901 the leading officials involved in the Boxer movement were punished. Yu-hsien was executed along with many others, while more were ordered to commit suicide. Between 31 July and 17 September the international forces withdrew from Peking, and on 7 September the Chinese authorities signed the Boxer Protocol to confirm their acceptance of the Twelve Demands. Reparation of 450 million *taels* (1 *tael* = three shillings) was demanded – a sum that represented more than twice China's annual public purse income.

As Reginald Fleming Johnston wrote his reports of the Boxer rebellion he was witnessing the beginning of developments that would alter for ever the traditional China he had entered. And the more he learned about the old ways the more he yearned to be a part of a fast-vanishing lifestyle. The glorious isolation of the Ch'ing Court of the Manchu dynasty was lost for ever. For example, the Empress Dowager was obliged to hold receptions for the wives of foreign diplomats when the court returned to the Forbidden City on 7 January 1902. And throughout the land scholars examined and questioned the archaic systems prevailing at all levels of Chinese life.

A direct consequence of the first Demand was to draw Johnston into the society of Chinese imperial affairs.[5] During the mid-morning of 25 July 1901, His Imperial Highness Tsai Feng, Prince Ch'un, brother of Emperor Kuang-hsu, landed with his entourage at the VIP pier at Hong Kong island from the 28,000-ton capital ship *Bayern* of the German High Seas Fleet. Johnston was one of the British welcoming party who escorted the prince in a ceremonial chair borne by a quartet of red-uniformed bearers to Government House. This was the first time that a Chinese prince had disembarked on British territory and it was a visit conducted without official fuss, at the prince's request, as he was on a 'mission of humility' to apologize for the murder of Baron von Ketteler. Prince Ch'un was received at Government House by Sir Henry Blake, and soon after left for Berlin.

Johnston prepared a memo for the Foreign Office bag concerning the visit. He remarked: 'Though Prince Ch'un cannot, according to the dynastic customs of China, himself become a candidate for the imperial throne, it is not impossible that if he has any children his son may eventually become emperor. This would certainly make Prince

Ch'un himself a very important factor in the future politics of China.'[6] His words foreshadowed actual events, but in his astute observation he could hardly have anticipated his own involvement in the consequences.

* * *

When the Russians withdrew their troops from Manchuria on 18 April 1902, Reginald Fleming Johnston realized that the conflict in China was calming down and decided to take some of his leave to explore more of mainland China and beyond. The region which interested him most were the territories that were opening up to British foreign diplomats in the south-west, where the British and French had made serious encroachments. At that time the British occupied Burma, which they had annexed in 1826, and parts of south-west China, and both north and south Siam (Thailand) were under their influence. The French held the region of Tongking as well as Laos, Cambodia, Annam and Cochin China as well as areas of south China to the north of Tongking and Kwangchow (modern Leizhou peninsula).

From Hong Kong Johnston travelled directly to Tongking, the name of the northern Mien Bao region of Vietnam in these French colonial times. This region contains the whole of the *Yuan Jiang* (Red River) plain, stretching from the slopes of the Truong San mountain chain to the Chinese border. The 750-mile long river passes Hanoi and flows to the Gulf of Tongking through a 50-mile wide delta. From here Johnston ascended the route into Yunnan, the second largest of China's provinces. Here the mountainous area embraces the western half of the Yungui Plateau and the great ranges and canyons of the southern Qan'do region. The surface of the plateau sports a mild temperate climate, whereas the south is subtropical to tropical. Johnston saw the bizarre scenery of the mountains, with the 'forest' of limestone crags, 100 feet high and pitted with caves, and a truly botanical paradise of some fifteen thousand plant species. In the foothills, too, the ethnic groups are related to several of the peoples of south-east Asia. Johnston traversed Yunnan from Geiju in the east to Dali in the west. The area had been popular with British consular staff (from Chungking) prospecting for trade since the late 1890s. The terrain was still somewhat risky for foreign travellers, being the scene of several murders of Christians some two decades before.

From Yunnan Johnston descended into Burma via the market town of Tengyueh. After Burma had become a lieutenant-governorship in 1897 the first British consulate had been opened at Tengyueh in 1899 under J.W. Jamieson, and the social life of the place had been enlivened by hunting. At Tengyueh Consul C.A.W. Rose hunted with a red setter and a pointer to fetch his kills, and set up a photographic darkroom at the consulate to indulge his hobby. Rose was a stickler for etiquette and dressed formally for cross-border meetings and wore a dinner jacket in the evening. To Johnston and other travellers he recommended that they carry a medicine bag containing quinine, Epsom salts, castor oil, iodine and embrocations, not only for their own use but as a useful form of barter with the local tribesfolk.[7]

Burma vegetated under the mellow glow of the *Pax Britannica* where the cultures of India and China meet. One of the longest rivers in Asia, the Salween, remains as untamed as the Shan jungles through which it sprints. In Johnston's day much of its length was unexplored and when the jungle tracts were first penetrated by the British, concealed in ambush were panthers, pythons, tigers and *dacoits* (bandits). In the vast river caves, with their huge, sinister-shaped stalactites and grisly rocks, the foetid air dampened the torches of early British explorers, and only the very brave teetered past the deep crevasses – down which dropped stones were never heard to land. Johnston was to delight in the folklore of the natives he encountered.[8] The Shan people and the hill Karens looked upon the Salween valley areas with fear and gave them a respectful wide berth because of their haunted reputation.

Johnston journeyed down the valley of the Salween River to the Chinese Shan States where oranges and Western vegetables flourished. In the Buddhist Shan States life slumbered in a kind of medieval timewarp which gave it a delightful Arcadian feel to the Edwardian traveller. From the Shan lands Johnston crossed the border into the French protectorate and explored Upper Laos before entering Siam and the capital, Bangkok.

During all his tours Johnston ran a considerable risk. For the most part he travelled alone, and even with bearers, he would make trips on his own to temples and sacred places. The most dangerous areas were the mountain regions and the disputed lands between states and along China's borders with her neighbours.

Although armed with a hunting rifle, Johnston faced the daily threat of kidnap by bandits. Wherever he travelled, there were hordes of dispossessed peasants and unemployed labourers, who holed up in inaccessible areas to live as outlaws. Throughout Chinese history, bandit groups had regularly composed the nuclei for peasant rebellions, such as that of the rebel leader Ch'en Sheng who was a factor in the downfall of the Ch'in Dynasty (221–207 BC).

Many trains were derailed by bandits, and in 1925 Johnston's friend H.G.W. Woodhead, editor of the *Peking and Tientsin Times*, was captured by sea-going bandits on his way to Weiheiwei. At his desk in Weiheiwei Johnston regularly had to process accounts of kidnappings of expatriates. It was his duty to warn travellers to the hinterland about bandit activity and to dissuade them from making certain trips. Johnston never took his own advice.

* * *

While his career was developing satisfactorily in China, the news from home was of the worst for Johnston. His father's declining health and economic position, coupled with his mother's profligacy, caused severe financial difficulties. The catalogue of embarrassment is confirmed in correspondence from Johnston to his friend, the Edinburgh lawyer R.A. Robertson. The extent of the economic catastrophe became clear after the death of Robert Fleming Johnston on 12 July 1902. A series of bad investments had undermined family funds and Johnston expressed dismay that his mother had to move from Goshen Bank to an 'inferior' part of Edinburgh. Until her death at the Queen Mary Nursing Home in Chalmers Street, Edinburgh, on 22 June 1916, at the age of 61, Johnston funded his mother, whose position always remained financially precarious as she in turn supported Noney's child.

Mrs Johnston lived a peripatetic life between various lodgings at Edinburgh and her daughter's shifting English addresses, and the number of pawn tickets redeemed on her death showed the extent of her frenetic spending. Johnston made it a matter of honour to pay off all his father's debts and his mother's bills. That was not all: despite the breakdown in good relations with his importuning mother – her letters to him in China became so abusive when he told her to economize that he refused to read them – Johnston also paid some debts accrued by his aunt Mrs Irving, who, he told Robertson, was one of the family who had married into a group of 'drunkards' and 'spendthrifts'.[9]

The news from home did not blunt Johnston's appetite for adventure; if anything it strengthened his enthusiasm for things Chinese. His notebooks teemed with jottings and trivia, from the appearance of the first motor cars in Shanghai in 1902 to the opening to traffic of the Chinese Eastern Railway in 1903.

In early February 1904 Russia and Japan declared war on each other over rights in Manchuria and Korea. Their war was to last until 5 September 1905 and despite Chinese neutrality it was a landmark in the modern history of China in particular, and in Asian and international relations in general. The war showed how the untried Japanese not only gained the victory but virtually annihilated Czarist Russia's sea power. For the first time in centuries an Oriental nation had defeated a major Western power.

Diplomatically, Japan was on friendly terms with Britain. An Anglo-Japanese alliance was in place by 1902 – to meet the threat of Russian expansion in the Far East – and remained in force until the close of 1921. Johnston was in a key position to observe the progress of Japanese influence through China. Japanese diplomats were to play an important role in Johnston's career as tutor to Emperor Pu Yi, but for the present he concentrated on a new posting in the offing.

At some time during the early years of the century Johnston had struck up a friendship with an important senior Colonial Office functionary. Sir James Haldane Stewart Lockhart was a fellow-Scot whose career as a Cadet had followed a similar pattern to Johnston's. Born at Ardsheal, by Loch Linnhe in Argyllshire, on 25 May 1858, Lockhart was to be recognized as a knowledgeable sinologist and respected colonial service officer. A product of George Watson's College and the University of Edinburgh, Stewart Lockhart had not graduated but chose to seek employment via the competitive examination of the Indian Civil Service. He was unsuccessful, and switched to those examinations for service in the Colonial Office. This time his efforts prevailed and in 1878 he was offered a cadetship at Hong Kong, taking up duties in late 1879 after training in civil service protocols and the rudiments of spoken Chinese.

In 1882, after further tuition in Cantonese, Stewart Lockhart progressed to become Clerk of Councils and Chief Clerk in the Colonial Secretary's office, a position which offered experience in how the colony was administered. His promotion was rapid through the Registrar General's department to Superintendent of Opium Revenue, to Assistant Colonial Secretary and Auditor General in 1883. Thence he became Acting Registrar General in 1884, an office concerned with Chinese interests in Hong Kong. In 1887 he became Registrar General.

Stewart Lockhart married Edith Louise Rider on 25 January 1889. During 1895 he became Colonial Secretary, and thus he was most senior official to the then Governor of Hong Kong, Sir William

Robinson. In April 1902 he took up duties as the first civil Commissioner of Weiheiwei, arriving in Hong Kong on 3 May.[10]

On the northern coast of Shantung Province (Ch'eng Shan Tsui), and commanding the entry to the Gulf of Pechili from the Yellow Sea is the 'City of the August Moon', Weihei Ch'eng; its 6-mile wide bay is sheltered by the island of Liukung-tao. Although British war vessels, the frigate *Alceste* and the sloop *Lyra*, had visited the bay in 1816, British interest in the area only came about when in November 1896 Germany used the pretext of the death of two priests, Nies and Henle, in Shantung to seize Kiaochou. This they leased from the Chinese in 1897/98. Nervous of Germany's intentions and Japanese rapaciousness, the Imperial Czarist Government sent warships to Port Arthur, which they in time leased. In Britain the Conservative Government of Robert Gascoyne-Cecil, 3rd Marquis of Salisbury, assumed that the international dismemberment of China was afoot. The Cabinet formed a collective resolve to secure Weiheiwei, despite the Admiralty's report that the anchorage's potential as a Royal Navy base was minimal. So on 1 July 1898, at the time Her Majesty's Government was securing the 99-year lease in the New Territories across from Hong Kong island, the Chinese Government leased to Britain some 285 square miles, including the old walled city of Weihei, with its population of two thousand, 'for as long as Port Arthur shall remain in the occupation of Russia'.[11]

In 1903 Stewart Lockhart made it known to the Colonial Office that he needed a replacement for one of his assistants at Weiheiwei, Robert Walter, who was about to go on leave. He indicated that Johnston would fit the bill. The Colonial Office was not particularly enamoured of Stewart Lockhart's choice and were always dubious about the cost of running Weiheiwei in any eventuality. At last, with the support of Sir Charles Lucas, assistant secretary at the Colonial Office, Johnston was seconded to Weiheiwei.

When Reginald Fleming Johnston arrived at Weiheiwei, the Stewart Lockharts and their children were established in the seven-roomed

Government House at Ma-t'ou, overlooking the bay. From his cramped quarters Stewart Lockhart had organized from scratch all the administration needed for the 150,000-strong population. Johnston took up residence at a house on the Bund at Port Edward, near Government House.

Johnston immediately worked on the background of his new posting.[12] In 1860 Weiheiwei had been visited by Lieutenant-General Sir James Hope Grant (1808–75), commander in the second Chinese war, 1860–61, who confirmed its location as of little importance to the Royal Navy. In 1895 the area was assaulted by Marshal Iwao Oyama's Second Army of the Imperial Nipponese Army by land and by Vice-Admiral Ito's five squadrons of the Imperial Nipponese Navy by sea, the latter destroying Admiral Ju-Ch'ang Ting's Peiyang Squadron of fifteen vessels. The Japanese remained in occupation of Weiheiwei until 1898 in accord with the Treaty of Shimonoseki.

The Chinese Regiment of Chinese nationals from Shantung, led by British officers, had been raised at Weiheiwei in early 1899 and served during the Boxer emergency.[13] Weiheiwei remained under the joint administration of the War Office and the Admiralty, under Sir A. Dorward as Commissioner, until 1901, when it was decided to administer it as a civil entity; the Colonial Office took over in May 1902 and the regiment was slowly disbanded.

Plans had been mooted to develop Weiheiwei as a naval base protected by a fortress harbour. The financing of the South African War scuppered such plans and in 1902 Her Majesty's Government announced, 'It is not the intention . . . to refortify the station, but to retain it as a flying naval base, and as a depot and drill-ground and sanatorium for the China Squadron in North China.'[14]

Nevertheless the British authorities developed some roads and wharfing in the 10-mile strip and three hundred settlements of their mandate and endeavoured to develop a 'picturesque resort' for holidaying residents in China who stayed at the King's Hotel or the newly-built bungalows.

With its administrative hub at Port Edward on Narcissus Bay, a mile or so from the Chinese city of Weihei, the centre of activity for Weiheiwei was the south-west corner of Liukung-tao and the northern shore of Narcissus Bay. Two golf courses, sulphur baths (run by Japanese interests), hunting and horseback explorations of the immediate countryside were available to entertain visitors, while the Stewart Lockharts at Government House held soirées for the Royal Navy officers and their wives and any visiting dignitaries. Ordinary ratings looked upon Weiheiwei as a depressing billet.

Johnston set about his new posting with a will, furthering his knowledge of Chinese. He spoke Cantonese fluently but now took up the study of the dialect prominent at Weiheiwei. Stewart Lockhart was confident enough in his new aide to entrust him with carrying out a ceremonial gesture. In 1903 Stewart Lockhart received a request from Duke K'ung for a picture of King Edward VII. K'ung lived at Ch'u-fu where Stewart Lockhart had met him on his first journey to Shantung.[15] The picture was duly ordered from London and Johnston escorted it, in its ornately embellished frame, and in its own carrying chair, to the Duke's palace. The powerful K'ung clan were direct descendants of the sage Confucius. Such was their influence that they had had the local railway line diverted from Ch'u-fu because its presence interfered with the *feng-shui* (geomantic harmony) of the area and would 'shake the tomb of the Sage' and cause the spirits of generations of K'ungs to be distressed.[16]

The seeds of the lifelong friendship between Stewart Lockhart and Johnston were nurtured during the absences of Mrs Lockhart and her children on their trips to Britain. Stewart Lockhart admired Johnston's devotion to scholarship, his keenness of interest in all things Chinese and his growing skills as a Chinese linguist. Madge Johnston remembered her parents talking about Stewart Lockhart and Johnston's 'mad trips' to temples for picnics, or overnight stays looked after by a cook and bearers.[17] Whenever he could, largely to relieve the boredom of routine administration, Johnston made trips into the Chinese countryside, and during his first year at Weiheiwei Johnston undertook his second major trip into the Chinese interior.

From Weiheiwei he went first to German-occupied Kiaochou. The German seat of government was at Tsingtau, at the entrance of Kiaochou Bay, in the area occupied by the Germans in 1897 and leased for ninety-nine years on 6 March 1898. (The area was actually lost to them during the First World War when it was besieged by the British and Japanese.) Johnston saw it as a superior location to Weiheiwei, with a large amount of money having been spent in improvements. The foreign residents' quarter was one of the finest in Asia. For Johnston, though, a highlight of his year was his trip to the tomb of Confucius.

From his early days in China, Johnston formed a great enthusiasm for Buddhism and was to write widely about it in books such as *Buddhist China*. The work is a sympathetic study which traces the early history of Buddhism in China and follows Buddhist pilgrim trails to the cult's sacred locations and ends with descriptions of the Buddhist monks and monasteries he encountered at Chiu Hua Shau and Puto Sha. His predilection for 'solitary walks' round temples and 'looking into space at Chinese sacred places' was to tar him with the brush of eccentricity among his colleagues.[18] Again his strengthening pro-Chinese sentiments caused some criticism among the missionaries of his acquaintance who saw him as increasingly 'anti-Christian'.

Johnston was now promoted to the post of Southern District Magistrate in a new division of administration responsibility at Weiheiwei. This gave him a staff of Chinese clerks and policemen and a remit to oversee some hundred thousand people. He noted that he undertook 'the duties of Registrar-General (Protector of Chinese), Puisne Judge, Police Magistrate and Captain-Superintendent of Police'.[19]

The countryside and people of China were a constant pull on Johnston's attentions and in 1906 he embarked – with his bull-terrier Jim – on his third great exploration of China. This was to result in his book *Peking to Mandalay*, which he dedicated to his Edinburgh tutor and friend David Playfair Heatley. In the introduction he averred that his trip was 'to gratify a long-felt desire to visit those portions of the Chinese Empire which are least known to Europeans and to acquire some knowledge of the various tribes subject to China that inhabit the wild regions of Chinese Tibet and north-western Yunnan'. An added attraction was that no British people had ever gone there.

He left Weiheiwei on 6 January 1906 aboard the steamer *Shuntian*, bound for Peking. In his book he describes his route from the capital to Ichang, the highest point, one thousand miles or so from the sea but accessible to ocean-going vessels. With the help of the British Consul there, H.H. Fox, Johnston procured a 'red boat' to take him through the famous Yangtze rapids and gorges and beyond, travelling cross-country from Wan-Hsien to Cheng Tu-Fu and the holy Buddhist mountain of Omeishan in Szechuan Province. Via Tachienlu in Tibetan China, where the British opened a consulate in 1913, he journeyed to the borders of eastern Tibet, and then descended through southern Yunnan through the Mekong Valley to Burma. He walked vast distances, supplementing his shoe leather with a dug-out canoe, rafts (on the Mekong), railways and steamers. Travelling mostly alone, ahead of his hired bearers, he would sometimes stay with missionaries – despite being a neophyte Buddhist – and at lamaseries and temples, or he would camp, with or without a tent.

Johnston left Rangoon on 19 July 1906 for a trip to Colombo as a guest of Sir Henry Blake, his erstwhile superior at Hong Kong, now Governor of Ceylon. From there he went on to Singapore, Hong Kong, Shanghai and Japan, spending two weeks in the southernmost main Nipponese island, Kyushu. By 5 October 1906 he was back in Weiheiwei and records with sadness the death of his bull-terrier Jim after their epic tour. On his travels Johnston saw a China that was just awakening 'from her old lethargy' to try 'to assert her independence and to repudiate foreign interference'. He had found his 'spiritual home'.

* * *

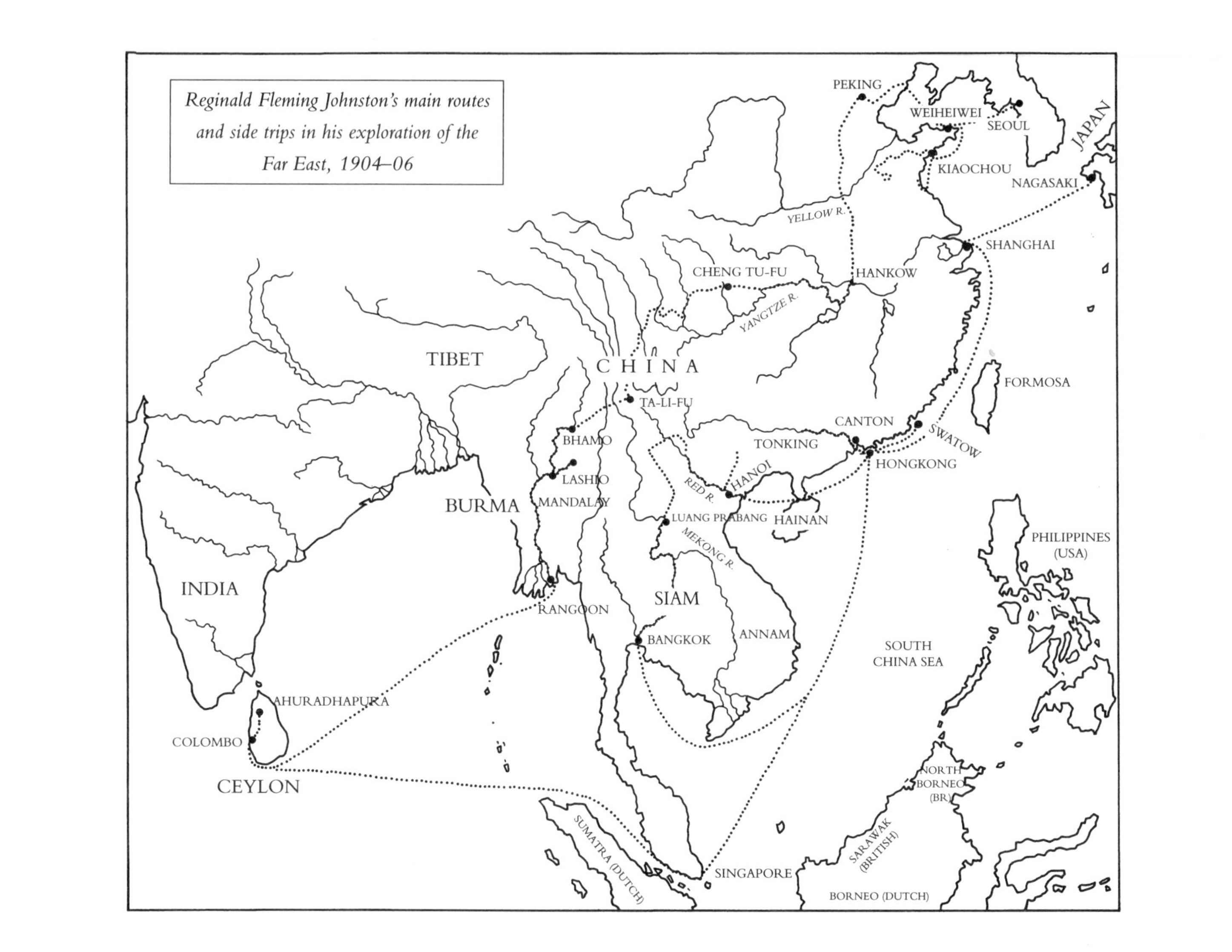

Reginald Fleming Johnston's main routes and side trips in his exploration of the Far East, 1904–06

Weiheiwei functioned against a backcloth of upheaval. On 5 September 1905 the Treaty of Portsmouth brought the Russo-Japanese War to an end and Chinese sovereignty in Manchuria was restored, but the Japanese took over the lease of the Liaodong peninsula and the Chinese Eastern Railway, previously held by Czarist Russia. Off the record both Johnston and Stewart Lockhart were delighted that Japan had been victorious during the war, but as the years went by Japan's rapacious attitude towards China was to cause dismay. On 31 August 1907 Britain and Russia recognized Chinese sovereignty in Tibet and on 2 December 1908 Johnston's future pupil Pu Yi was declared Emperor of China.

As the years of the Edwardian Empire passed away, Johnston became more sinophile, adopting a Chinese way of life, at least in his domestic arrangements. Yet his 'Scottishness' was indulged from time to time in the events of the Weiheiwei St Andrew's Society, and his penchant for sailing was probably engendered at the same time; this was to be a solace during his retirement in Scotland.[20] Thoughts of Scotland were somewhat bittersweet, as they brought back the memory of his mother's extravagance which so drained the allowance he sent her regularly. In 1907 he wrote to his mother that because of her any thoughts he had of marriage were out of the question as he could not afford to support a wife.[21] All the while, though, he was adding to his knowledge of China and he studied Mandarin to help him understand the extant books of Chinese literature, and there was a growing restlessness to move on in his career.

* * *

From his first days at Weiheiwei, Johnston had filled many notebooks with his jottings, and in 1904 he produced his *Account of a Journey in Shantung from Weiheiwei to the Tomb of Confucius* and *Remarks on the Province of Shantung*. Johnston's writings were not confined to prose: for years he had dabbled with verse. Back in 1904 he had paid Blackwells of Oxford to publish his curiously titled volume of poems *The Last Days of Theodoric the Ostrogoth*, highlighting his lead poem. In the slim book were lines he had written in his early teenage years, the earliest being dated 1891, when he was seventeen. Some he dedicated (by initials) to his old friend David Playfair Heatley and Magdalen contemporaries Clementi, Armitage and Loveday, with whom he had shared jaunts to such places as Bonshaw Tower, Dumfriesshire, in the land of the Flemings and the Johnstons.

In 1910 Johnston's book *Lion and Dragon in Northern China* was published by John Murray. This, and his other writings, he hoped would ease some of the financial burdens caused by his mother and would also fund his own research trips into China's hinterland. In the book he deals in a thorough manner with Weiheiwei and uses the physical and historical environments to interpret the folklore of the place. Herein too, Johnston introduces the western reader to the subtleties of *feng-shui* (geomancy). The book remains an undoubted labour of love but coded within were two trains of thought which can be added to the key clues to Johnston's character.

He devotes vital pages to a trenchant protest against criticisms of Confucianism. His impatience with anyone who criticized China was to grow as years passed, and from this time his hankering for the old China – which was to be almost eradicated in his lifetime – became an obsession: it made him blind to the changes in China's political reality.

The book also reveals Johnston's interest in Japan's role in China – raping the people and annexing territory in the headlong descent to the horrors of the Second World War. In the future Johnston's interest in Japan was frequently taken as pro-Japanese leanings; his future close dealings with them, in the case of Pu Yi's flight to their Legation, brought Johnston façe to face with their deviousness as diplomats in China, something he chose to ignore.

Soon after the publication of *Lion and Dragon in Northern China* his mind turned to poetry writing again, and the perusal of what he had published in his volume of 1904 under the title of 'Love's Devotion':

I would that I were strong and pure and wise;
Then mightst thou take me to thy heart and love me.
But who am I to win so great a prize?
I love in vain: thou art far above me.

Today I gazed upon thee silently:
Rapt in high thought thou passed by unheeding.
If thou had'st known, thou mightst have sighed for me,
But how wast thou to guess my heart was bleeding?

How couldst thou see that I did love thee so?
I gave no sign to show the heart's emotion.
I turned mine eyes away, lest they might show
The passionate secret of a soul's devotion.

Enough for me to know thee as thou art,
Of all God's creatures purest, noblest, fairest.
I cannot help but give thee all my heart
Although thou hast no thought for me nor carest.

I would not have thee waste a thought on me;
I would not have thy love bestowed so cheaply;
Though my best joy will still be loving thee,
Love's best reward, the power to love more deeply.

The inspiration for further amatorial verses was his falling in love with a girl seventeen years his junior, the twenty-year-old, dark-eyed Edwardian beauty, Alice Walter. In a pencilled adjunct to the *Moore Papers* Kitty Moore wrote:

[Johnston] seemed to be smitten with [Alice] from the first. She was always smiling, her brown eyes sparkling with mischief as she teased and flirted with the young men at the Commissioner's picnics.

> Those who first met her in the summer of 1911, when she became a firm friend of Betty Lockhart [a daughter of Commissioner Lockhart], remarked at her very pale skin; no wonder they teased her with the nickname 'Camille'. [The character Marguerite Gauthier in Alexandre Dumas's *La Dame aux Camélias*, 1852.]
>
> The Lockharts were generous hosts and Reggie's romance with Alice developed through the round of dinners, musical evenings, beach picnics, and shooting parties. A great treat for us all was to have jaunts on the Commissioner's yacht where Reggie always seemed to be just by Alice's elbow lest she miss her footing.
>
> None of the women doubted that Alice was in love with Reggie. When he turned on the charm most women were fascinated by him. He had a wonderful sense of humour and a whole range of nicknames for people he met, particularly the colonial officers and military and naval men who came to Weiheiwei. Reggie started to give little tennis parties at his own quarters overlooking the bay and Alice was always there.

It seems that Alice Walter had visited Weiheiwei just for the summer season, but she stayed on. Kitty Moore was one who watched the romance develop: 'We never knew if Reggie had popped the question – everyone expected him to do so. I left Weiheiwei at the end of the year so I was behind with the gossip for a while. So, I was surprised to get Charlie's letter [her husband] in which he said that Alice had returned to Europe.'

What happened to the relationship between Johnston and Alice Walter remains a mystery. In 1913, though, she seems to have gone to Paris. Johnston wrote to her from time to time and received replies, but in Europe she met a naval officer and married him. It is known that she arrived in Shanghai with her husband in 1919, the year that Johnston became the emperor's tutor.

* * *

During 1911, as a result of a republican uprising which began in Hangchow, the dynasty of the Manchus was overthrown and Nanking was made the national capital. On 1 January 1912 the Republic of China was proclaimed, with revolutionary Dr Sun Yat-sen (1866–1925) as provisional president, and on 12 February Emperor Pu Yi issued his edict of abdication. The events saddened the traditionalists Stewart Lockhart and Johnston and the latter wrote to his friend R.A. Robertson that his life was taken up with fending off 'bandits and pirates' from the British borders at Weiheiwei.[22]

As these events rumbled on, Reginald Fleming Johnston had engendered his own 'revolutionary thoughts' against the Christian missionaries in China. Following the Treaty of Nanking in 1842 an increased number of foreign missionaries started to enter China and thousands were to die for their tenacity and zeal in various upsurges of xenophobia. Johnston formed an early antipathy towards missionaries – particularly American ones, their methods and infiltration. In 1911 he published his first diatribe against the missionary societies in *A Chinese Appeal to Christendom Concerning Christian Missions*. It appeared under the pen name *Lin Shao-Yang*. Its publication caused theologians like Dr H.T. Hodgkin, an erstwhile resident of Chengtu, to challenge its authorship as Chinese.[23] Johnston was to keep the anti-missionary pot boiling with his *Letters to a Missionary* (1918). He believed that his views had altered 'some of the crudities of evangelical mission-work in China'[24] but that they had also cost him the future governorship of Hong Kong and the Vice-chancellorship of Hong Kong University.[25]

In 1913 Johnston was unsettled with his service and took long leave to return to Britain to review his future. On visiting the Colonial Office he was treated indifferently and saw no future for himself in the Colonial Service. In a letter to Stewart Lockhart, dated 26 December, from his lodgings at Ealing, he notes that he is to see his friend and old Edinburgh tutor David Playfair Heatley concerning a proposed Chair of Chinese at Edinburgh University for himself.[26] Writing again from the Royal Societies Club, London, on 5 January 1914, Johnston admitted that after spending some time with Heatley the Edinburgh chair was not likely to be a reality.[27] He returned to China aboard the P&O vessel *Malta*, hoping for an extension of leave to indulge in more travel, but his application was refused. However, there was news that Sir George Macartney, HM Consul-general at Kashgar, Afghanistan, was about to retire. Stewart Lockhart (Sir James since the award of the KCMG in 1908) suggested Johnston for the post, thus persuading him not to resign from the service. However, the outbreak of the First World War caused Macartney to be stuck in Afghanistan, and Johnston's chance was lost.

Johnston sat out the war, carrying on his duties, and with Stewart Lockhart's knowledge petitioned the Colonial Office about his lack of advancement. Johnston's reputation as a Chinese scholar, however, was recognized in 1916, when he and Stewart Lockhart were both awarded honorary degrees by Hong Kong University.[28] In 1918 Johnston was awarded the CBE.

At the end of the war Johnston again spent his leave travelling to the interior of China. It is known from his letters to Stewart Lockhart that he applied unsuccessfully for the Chair of Chinese at Columbia University in America at the end of 1917,[29] and for the Vice-Chancellorship of Hong Kong University.[30] By the end of October 1918 he was sojourning at Shanghai to see old friends, studying the latest Chinese academic papers at the Royal Asiatic Society library there – and conducting a meeting that would change his life.

He was approached in Shanghai by one Li Ching-mai, a prominent courtier of the now imploded Manchu dynasty. Li was the son of Viceroy Li Hung-chang and Johnston had met him at Weiheiwei during the courtier's flight from the turmoil at Peking. At a dinner party on 26 October Li invited Johnston to meet him the next day to discuss a subject of great moment. It seemed that the current President of China, Hsu Shih-ch'ang, was anxious to groom the still extant emperor – although he had abdicated – for a time when he could be presented to the Chinese people as a constitutional monarch. The plan was long term but vital.

The immediate task, though, was to educate the young emperor in subjects such as political science, constitutional history and English, the language of international intercourse. President Hsu Shih-ch'ang, a former imperial tutor himself, knew precisely the manner of candidate who would fit the bill – and that man was Reginald Fleming Johnston.

Li Ching-mai had researched Johnston's background and was fully satisfied of his fitness for the position of imperial tutor. With President Hsu Shih-ch'ang's authority Johnston was informally offered the job. The formal offer was to be issued through the Office of the President of the Republic to the Office of the British Minister at Peking. Loyal to Stewart Lockhart, Johnston told his old friend and boss about the offer: did Stewart Lockhart want the job himself? No, and Johnston would be the ideal man for the role. The Foreign Office was approached and offered no objection; indeed, they were keen that an American was *not* appointed, in order to avoid the increase of US influence in a court that might yet be resuscitated. Johnston now prepared for the position that would make him internationally famous.[31]

CHAPTER 3

IMPERIAL PUPIL: ENTRANCE OF THE SON OF HEAVEN

Reginald Fleming Johnston's imperial pupil owed his position to the *T'ai-hou* (Empress Dowager) Tzu Hsi, widow of the dissolute Ch'ing Dynasty Emperor Hsien-feng (r. 1851–61) and mother of her husband's childless successor T'ung Chih (r. 1862–74).[1] Born in 1835 as *Lan Kuei* (Little Orchid) before receiving her imperial title, Tzu Hsi dominated China from 1860 until her death. When Emperor Hsien-feng died, Tzu Hsi and the senior imperial concubine T'z'u-an became important advisers to the regency of her five-year-old son. Eventually the two women overthrew the regency and formed their own ruling power with Tzu Hsi as the dominant partner. When the dual-regency ended in 1873 Emperor T'ung Chih continued to be dominated by his mother and on his death she installed her three-year-old nephew Kuang-hsu as emperor. He was not in the line of succession but through his person Tzu Hsi could continue to control the court. In 1889 she gave up control of state affairs and retired to the Summer Palace, to the north-west of Peking, but frequently came into conflict with Kuang-hsu – dubbed the 'Prisoner Emperor' because of her influence – and in 1898 she directly intervened to prevent the success of the Hundred Days Reform.

Known as the 'wickedest woman in the world' to foreign diplomats, Tzu Hsi was the most vain, xenophobic, merciless, devious and unscrupulous ruler of her generation. She was the embodiment of all that was corrupt, immoral and misguided in China's ruling hierarchy of the nineteenth century. Yet her strong personality, manipulative dexterity and skill in confounding her enemies drew reluctant admiration from the international chancelleries in China.[2]

Referred to more properly by the epithets *Lao Tsu Tsung* (Venerable Ancestor) or *Lao Fo-yen* (Venerable Buddha), Tzu Hsi placed Johnston's imperial pupil Pu Yi on the throne of China two days before her death. She had published her Imperial Decree for this on 13 November 1908 – one day before the demise of the Emperor Kuang-hsu. This document was unprecedented in the history of Chinese Imperial succession. In the language of the court it read:

> The Emperor T'ung Chih, having left no heir, is compelled to issue a Decree to the effect that as soon as a child should be born to His Majesty the Kuang-hsu Emperor, that child would be adopted as heir to the said T'ung Chih Emperor. But now His Majesty the Kuang-hsu Emperor has ascended on high, dragon-borne, and he has also left no heir. I am, therefore, now obliged to decree that Pu Yi, son of Tsai Feng [Prince Ch'un], 'Prince cooperating in the government', should become heir by adoption to the T'ung Chih Emperor, and that, at the same time, he should perform joint sacrifices at the shrine of His Late Majesty the Kuang-hsu Emperor.[3]

The Decree formally, if prematurely, announced the death of Emperor Kuang-hsu. Many believed that he had been murdered on the orders of Tzu Hsi, fearful that he might outlive her and expose her infamous machinations which would compel her soul at death to wander the Great Darkness before reaching the Nine Springs of Eternal Life. In more recent times fingers have pointed more confidently to General Yuan Shih-k'ai, counsellor and controller of the Chinese Army, as the probable murderer. He had his own candidate for the Dragon Throne in Prince Pu Lun, grandson of Emperor Tao-Kuang (r. 1821–50) and great-nephew of the dying emperor – a choice dismissed by Tzu Hsi who had already been warned by her chief eunuch Li Lien-ing that Yuan was planning to murder the emperor. Yet fate decreed that the emperor's death on 14 November 1908 was followed the next day by that of Tzu Hsi.[4]

Having returned from his mission to Germany in 1901 to expiate the murder of Baron von Ketteler, Prince Ch'un was married off by Tzu Hsi to a daughter of Viceroy and Grand-counsellor Jung Lu. Writing in 1934 Reginald Fleming Johnston had this to say of Prince Ch'un:

> [He] was, and is, a man of some amiable qualities, free from malice or vindictiveness, sociable, as interested in the Chinese drama as he is uninterested in politics or in the affairs of the great world. He must be given credit for being one of the two Manchu princes (Tsai-hsun is the other) who has a respectable knowledge of the Manchu language. He is well-intentioned, tries in his languid and ineffectual way to please everyone, succeeds in pleasing no one, shrinks from responsibility, is thoroughly unbusinesslike, is disastrously deficient in energy, will-power and grit, and there is reason to believe that he lacks both physical and moral courage. He is helpless in an emergency, has no original ideas, and is liable to be swayed by any smooth talker. After he became regent, however, the flattery of sycophants tended to make him obstinately tenacious of his own opinions, which invariably turned out to be wrong. During several years of fairly intimate contact with Prince Ch'un I came to be so deeply impressed by his fatal tendency to do the wrong thing or choose the wrong course in matters affecting the Imperial House or the interests of the young emperor his son, that I once made the suggestion to my colleagues in the Forbidden City that we might actually turn that tendency of his to good account by adopting the following general principle: If two possible courses of action presented themselves, ask Prince Ch'un which in his opinion should be followed – then follow the other.[5]

Pu Yi was born at the Ch'un family home of *Pei Fu* ('Northern Mansion'), in the old Tartar district of Peking on the 14th Day of the First Moon of the 32nd Year of the Emperor Kuang-hsu's reign: 7 February 1906. His grandfather Yi-huan, first Prince Ch'un, was the seventh son of Emperor Tao Kuan, while Pu Yi's father, Tsai Feng, the second Prince Ch'un, was the brother of Emperor Kuang-hsu. Grandfather Prince Ch'un had been a loyal supporter of the Empress Dowager, so Pu Yi inherited the favours of dynastic precedence.

For Pu Yi the bewildering journey from the nursery to imperial immortality began on the evening of 13 November 1908 when a procession of imperial cavalry, headed by the Imperial Palace Chamberlain and acolyte dignitaries, paused with a palanquin, borne by eunuchs, outside the *Pei Fu* mansion. As the cavalry halted by the lake, the palanquin was carried through the gates of the Northern Mansion, and as it arrived Prince Ch'un realized that the Empress Dowager was fast approaching death and had sent for Pu Yi as her successor.

As the chamberlain entered, the three-year-old Pu Yi was being entertained by his twenty-year-old wet nurse Wan Chao. He was used to his home being full of relatives, attendants and sycophants, but the mêlée caused by the arrival of the imperial entourage caused the wilful, disobedient child to panic. As the chamberlain ordered him to be dressed in warm clothes for his journey, the terrified Pu Yi fled from his nurse's arms to hide in a cupboard. At last the eunuch attendants prised him howling and wriggling from his haven and he was placed in his nurse's soothing arms in the palanquin. His mother – whom he would not see again for six years – had fainted and his father sat stunned. The gods would not be pleased, witnesses of the events averred, at this disruptive start to the new reign.

As the snow fell silently over the roofs of Peking, little Pu Yi entered a strange new world. The Forbidden City was like a Chinese puzzle box, a city within a city within a city. Its thousands of inhabitants lived in a myriad sealed palace complexes, gardens, temples, streets and courtyards, mirroring the centuries of insularity favoured by China's rulers. The daily life in each living area was designed to be veiled in secrecy and every nook and cranny was conducive to the Chinese passion for intrigue. The city was the seat of the entire government of China, with a complex of armouries, schools, banks, prisons, theatres, kennels and art stores.

Surrounded by a 32ft high wall and a 160ft wide moat, the Imperial Palace still stands at the entrance of the Forbidden City. The complex was deemed to have a range of 9,999 rooms, all within an interlocking design of pavilions, courtyards, alleys and towers. Each tower and pavilion had its own individuality; the double-roofed tower for the emperor's own use was glazed in tiles of imperial yellow, while the Phoenix Pavilion, with its effigies of China's mythological bird of good fortune, was one of the most splendid. The palace is connected to the core of the Forbidden City by the *Chinshi Ch'iao* ('Golden Water Bridge') with its imperial central walkway leading to the Gate of Supreme Harmony and the courtyard for the assemblies of the 90,000 officials.

Nineteen other palaces were set within the grounds of the Forbidden City, all living quarters for the emperors' wives, dowagers, concubines and eunuchs. By Pu Yi's day the thousands of eunuchs had been reduced to two hundred, but these castrated careerists still exerted enormous influence, the complexity and corruption of which had helped Tzu Hsi achieve her position and plunder the state's wealth.

Soon after alighting from the gold and mahogany palanquin that had brought him to the Forbidden City, Pu Yi was carried by Wan Chao to the Hall of Mental Cultivation to meet his great-aunt the Empress Dowager. Pu Yi left this memory of the occasion:

> I still have a dim recollection of the meeting, the shock of which left a deep impression on my memory. I remember suddenly finding myself surrounded by strangers, while before me was hung a drab curtain through which I could see an emaciated and terrifyingly

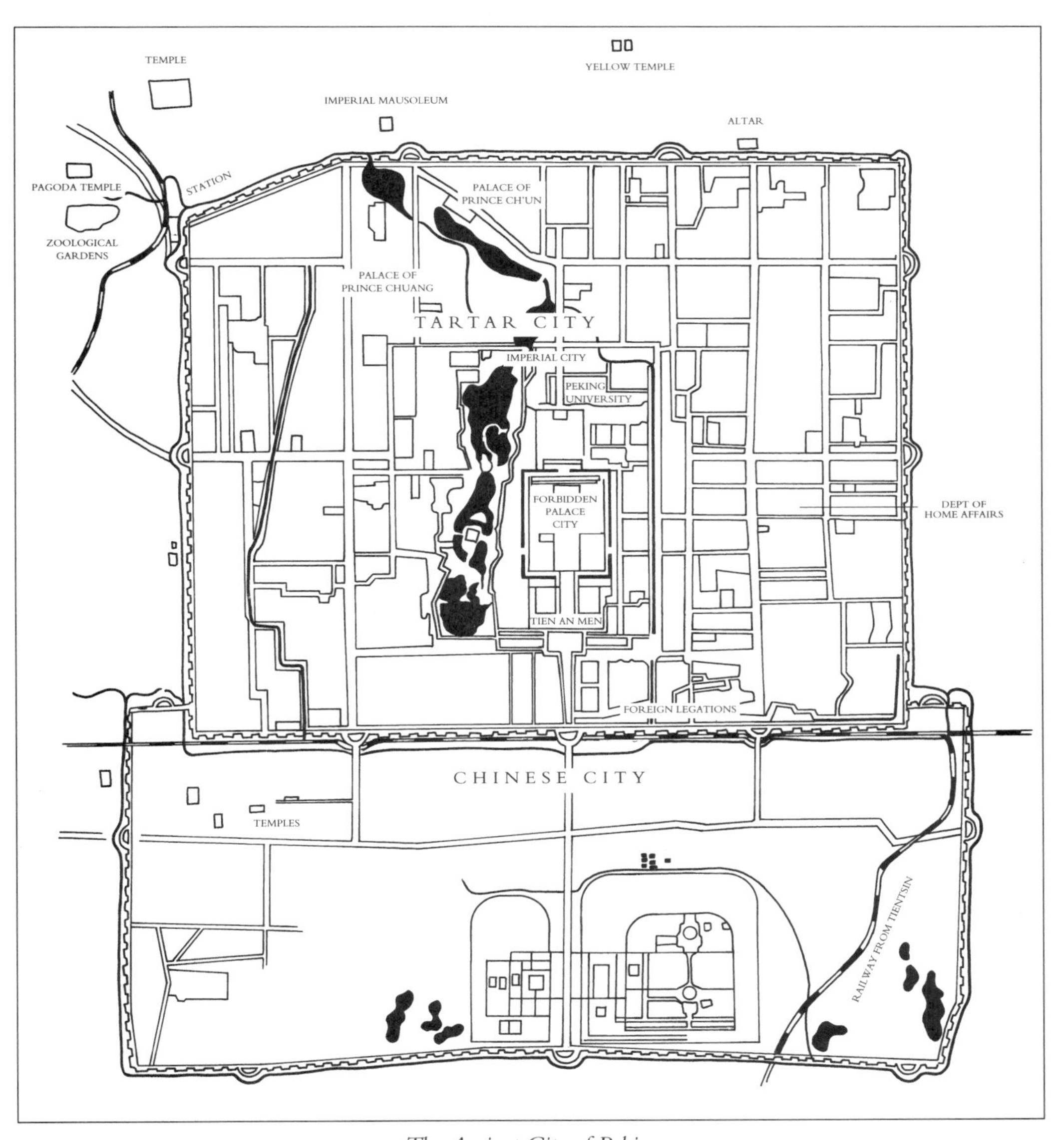

The Ancient City of Peking

The Forbidden City, built between 1406 and 1420 within the centre of modern Beijing city proper, was the imperial residence of twenty-four emperors of the Ming and Ch'ing (1644–1911) dynasties. The Forbidden City lay at the core of the Imperial City, surrounded by the old Tartar City, and the whole lay to the north of the ancient Chinese City. Today the Forbidden City is one of the largest and best preserved palace complexes in the world. It became the Palace Museum in the 1950s and contains around a million rare artefacts. Set with yellow tiles over red walls, gilded doors behind vermilion colonnades, with carved white marble balustrades around, the palace halls in their symmetrical design represent the height of China's ancient architectural skills.

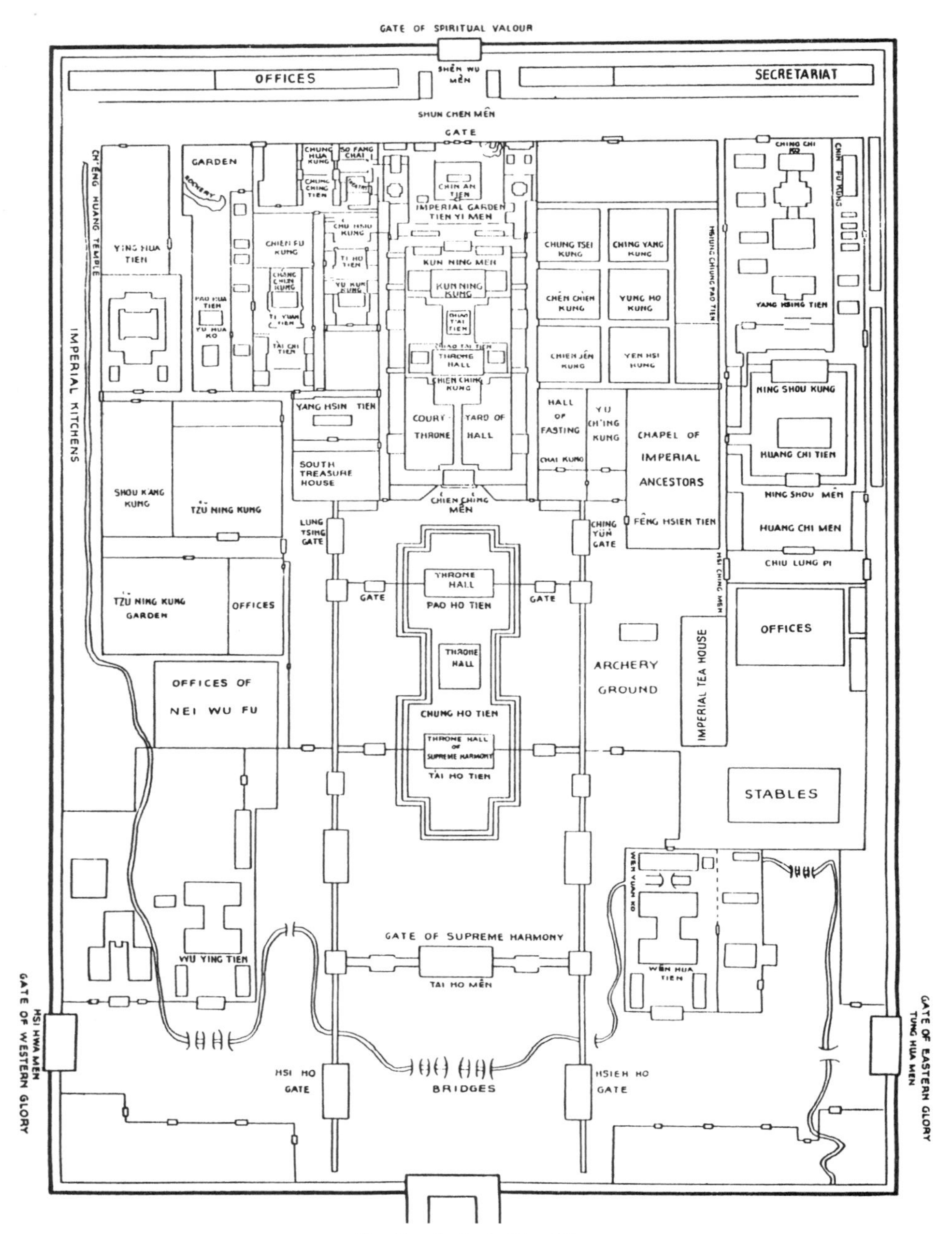

The Purple Forbidden City
The Throne Hall – Hall of Supreme Harmony – is China's tallest ancient palace building of timber where from 1644 to 1911 all the important national ceremonies took place.

Key Features of The Purple Forbidden City 1908–24

Wu-ying Tien *Wen-hua Tien*	Former palaces. Museums for the Imperial Collection, mostly artefacts from the palaces of Mukden, Manchuria, and Jehol
T'ai Ho Tien *Chung Ho Tien* *Pao Ho Tien*	[Hall of Supreme Harmony] Four throne halls used by the Republican Government
Ch'ien Ch'ing Kung	[Palace of Heavenly Purity] Preserve of the Emperor. Here great court occasions were held in buildings and the quadrangle
Yu Huan Yuan	Imperial Garden. Here Johnston first introduced the game of tennis, 20 October 1923. Site of Johnston's grace and favour mansion the *Yang Hsing Chai* [Lodge of the Nourishment of Nature] after 1924
Wen Yuan Ko	Pavilion for a portion of the Imperial Library
Nei Wu Fu	Office of the Imperial Household Department
Chun Chi Ch'ui	Office of the Grand Council of State
Chien Fu Kung	[Palace of Established Happiness] Destroyed by fire 1923
Feng Hsien Tien	[Chapel of Serving the Ancestors] Here the Emperor, his family and clan members, carried out memorial rites to the imperial ancestors on the 1st and 15th of the lunar month
T'ai Miao	[Supreme Temple] Here the Spirit Tablets of the Imperial Ancestors were kept
Shang Shu-fang	Office of Prince Ch'un, 1909–12
Mou-ch'un-tien	[Hall of Industrious Energy] Used by courtiers
Nan-shu-fang	[Southern Study] Used by courtiers
Chian-t'ai Tien	[Hall of the Blending of Great Creative Forces] Here divine spirits and earthbound forces were deemed to meet in creative harmony. Store for the Twenty-five Imperial Seals and the past empresses' gold-engraved *Ts'e Pao* [marriage certificates]
K'un-ning Kung	[Palace of Tranquil Earth] Manchu spirit rites
Yang-Hsin Tien	[The Mind Nurture Palace] The Emperor's own palace. Rebuilt 1802
Wu-ying Wen-hua	Palaces made into museums by the Republican Government
Yu-Ch'ing Kung	[Palace of the Bringing-Forth of Blessings] Palace where Johnston conducted the Emperor's lessons from 1919

> hideous face. This was Tzu Hsi. It is said that I burst out into loud howls at the sight and started to tremble uncontrollably . . . Tzu Hsi told somebody to give me some sweets, but I threw them on the floor and yelled: 'I want nanny, I want nanny', to [the empress's] great displeasure. 'What a naughty child,' she said. 'Take him away.'[6]

When Tzu Hsi died two days after Pu Yi's traumatic glimpse of her a wave of euphoria swept through the Forbidden City and beyond as the court prepared for Pu Yi's elevation to the Dragon Throne. On a cold 2 December 1908 Pu Yi was formally created spiritual and secular ruler of China *Da Ch'ing Da Huang Ti* ('Great Emperor of the Great Ch'ing Dynasty'). His Great Ceremonial Enthronement took place in the *Tai Ho Tien* ('Hall of Supreme Harmony'), with its seventy-two vermilion-painted columns, immediately following the obeisance of the commanders of the Palace Guard and the leading ministers and civil and military dignitaries at the *Chung Ho Tien* ('Hall of Central Ceremony').

The infant Pu Yi, now Son of Heaven, Lord of Ten Thousand Years, was given the *nien-hao* ('reign name') of Hsuan-t'ung, but as was customary he was given no *miao-hao* ('temple name'). In the chronicles of imperial history Pu Yi's clan was confirmed as *Aisin Gioro* ('Golden Race') and in everyday speech he had to become used to being addressed as *Huang shang* ('His Imperial Majesty'). Throughout the ceremony Pu Yi voiced his discomfort and recalled years later:

> I found it all long and tiresome. It was so cold that when they carried me into the Hall and perched me on the high and enormous throne I could bear it no longer. My father, who was kneeling below the throne supporting me, told me not to fidget, but I struggled and cried: 'I don't like it here. I want to go home.' My father grew so desperate he was pouring with sweat. As the officials went on kowtowing to me my cries grew louder and louder. My father tried to soothe me by saying, 'Don't cry, it'll soon be over.'[7]

Aged courtiers looked upon the infant emperor's shrieks and unruliness in the face of court dignity as an ill-omen for the success of the reign.

Pu Yi's life was transformed. He had become a living god to the imperial courtiers. His childhood vanished and he could only be a baby with his nurse Wan Chao, whose breast to suckle was his only comfort as she got him off to sleep in his rooms at the *Ch'ien-Ch'ing Kung* ('Palace of Heavenly Purity').

Poorly qualified and ungroomed for office, Pu Yi's father Prince Ch'un assumed the prescribed duties of Regent according to the Decree. He was never to settle into the position with any confidence but he became less of a shadowy figure to his son whom he had virtually ignored since birth. Yet Prince Ch'un was only to visit Pu Yi briefly every two months, and the nervous child never plucked up courage to speak to him more than a syllable or two. Pu Yi was to learn years later that his father had been weighed down by the duties of Regent and would much have preferred to have pursued his passion for astronomy.

From 1908 to 1911 Pu Yi lived in isolation within the *Da Nei* ('Great Within') of the Purple Forbidden City without any friends of his own age. Sometimes the unnaturalness of his surroundings promoted terrible tantrums, and his eunuch attendants were forced to lock him in a small punishment chamber until his frustrated emotions subsided. His only calming influence remained Wan Chao, who suckled him in his misery until he was eight years old.

Pu Yi's education, begun by the eunuch Chang Chieng-lo, concentrated on reading, writing and calligraphy and the recognition of the special Chinese characters used in all things imperial. Court rules laid down that the emperor should be fluent in Manchu – a language different from the Chinese spoken outside the Forbidden City – but Pu Yi never became fluent in it. He learned nothing of geography, science or mathematics, subjects replaced by Chinese classics and Confucian texts. Eventually a small schoolroom was set up at the *Yu Ching* ('The Palace of the Cultivation of Happiness'), and a few aristocratic children, including his younger brother Pu Chieh, joined him for his lessons. As emperor he could not be tested or chastised for errors and a whipping boy was selected to take the schoolroom beatings on his behalf. The choice was Yu Chung, son of Prince Pu Lun, who had been passed over as heir apparent in favour of Pu Yi.

The boy emperor's daily routine involved a visit to his five 'mothers' who lived in the Eastern Palaces of the Forbidden City. They were the widows, or former concubines, of the two preceding emperors. Their leader was Pu Yi's father's cousin, Princess Jung Shu (1854–1911), niece and adopted daughter of Tzu Hsi and Number One Wife of the late Emperor Kuang-hsu. She modelled herself on her aunt and became a feared tartar. Three of the other 'mothers' were dowager concubines of Emperor T'ung Chih, while the fourth was Lustrous Concubine, sister of the murdered Pearl Concubine of Emperor Kuang-hsu who had been sent to her fate by Tzu Hsi.

Pu Yi loathed Jung Shu. She was principally responsible for his beloved Wan Chao being ultimately expelled from the Forbidden City without his knowledge or a last farewell. Wan Chao was an illiterate country girl whom the imperial courtiers came to fear and hate. In her selfless devotion to Pu Yi she was seen to wield great influence over him which might, courtiers averred, lead to her in turn being manipulated by cadres for political purposes. So she had to go. Pu Yi was desolate.

From time to time Pu Yi gave audiences while sitting on his father's knee on the Dragon Throne. His life was cocooned by a thousand years of court protocol. But while all was calm in the Forbidden City, outside there was a groundswell of national unrest. Civil war had rumbled away in China since the Boxer Rebellion. In the south republicans were in the ascendant, led by the exiled revolutionary Dr Sun Yat-sen, founder in 1905 of the *Tung-meng hui* ('United Party') later to be absorbed into the *Kuomintang* ('Chinese National Party'). Parts of China, like Canton and Kwangtung Province, no longer recognized imperial administration and as Pu Yi played with Wan

Chao in the *Yu Hua Yuan* ('Imperial Garden') the collapse of the dynasty was already well advanced.

In early 1909 a decree was issued noting that the Imperial Court was committed to the setting up of a constitutional government. Those who opposed the decree were dismissed (or punished). One of Pu Yi's uncles, Tsai-Hsun, was sent to Britain heading a mission to study the Royal Navy with a view to establishing a modern Chinese navy. His brother, Tsai-T'ao, was sent on a similar, but military, mission to Germany; they were received with courtesy by King Edward VII and his nephew Kaiser Wilhelm II respectively.

Petitions for the proposed new parliament to open were now being received regularly by Prince Ch'un, and an edict was issued on 4 November 1909 that the parliament would be opened in 1913. This rate of progress was too slow for the reformers, and in 1910 one Wang Ching-wei (a follower of Dr Sun Yat-sen) made an unsuccessful assassination attempt on Prince Ch'un. The Regent foolishly commuted the death sentence passed on Wang to life-imprisonment, thus assuring Wang's future career as a leader of the Kuomintang and a member of the National Government at Nanking.

In one of the ironies of Chinese history, Pu Yi's reign was further undermined by his incompetent father. Prince Ch'un sacked the albeit devious General Yuan Shih-k'ai, who could have helped keep Imperial China as a Manchu entity. Yuan, a consummate poltroon, had betrayed the reformers of 1898 and had carefully consolidated his career for a decade and more; by 1901 he was appointed Viceroy of the Metropolitan Province; in 1903 he became Minister of the Army Reorganisation Council, and in 1907 President of the Board of Foreign Affairs and Grand Counsellor, all the while cultivating the Empress Dowager.

The real end of Pu Yi's dynasty came on 10 October 1911, when a group of young army officers at Wuhan mutinied for reform against corrupt senior officers. From Wuhan the revolt spread over most of China and Sun Yat-sen's republicans assumed leadership of the insurrection. On all sides, financiers, shopkeepers, soldiers and wealthy landowners clamoured for the removal of the archaic Manchus and their corrupt and grossly inefficient Ch'ing Dynasty.

Panicking, Prince Ch'un summoned the sacked Yuan Shih-k'ai back to Peking. In the meantime the ambitious Yuan, tempted with the carrot of being the first republican President of the neophyte *Ching Hua Min Kuo* ('Republic of China'), had been plotting with the revolutionaries. Although vacillating at Prince Ch'un's summons, Yuan ceased command of the imperial forces and went through the motions of defending the Manchu interests while ensuring the republicans were not confounded.

In December 1911 Prince Ch'un resigned as Regent and the Empress Dowager Jung Shu appointed Yuan to negotiate with the republicans. Although he was only five years old at the time, Pu Yi was later able to describe the scene that heralded the end of his reign:

> The Empress Dowager was sitting on a *kang* [platform bed] in a side room of the *Yang-Hsin Tien* [Mind Nurture Palace – Pu Yi's own palace], wiping her eyes with a handkerchief while a fat old man [Yuan Shih-k'ai] knelt on a red cushion before her, tears rolling down his face. I was sitting to the right of the Dowager and wondering why two adults were crying. There was nobody in the room besides us three and it was very quiet; the fat man was sniffing loudly while he talked and I could not understand what he was saying . . . This was the occasion Yuan directly brought up the question of abdication. After this meeting Yuan made the excuse that an attempt had been made on his life not to come to the court again.[8]

Yuan's crocodile tears marked his betrayal of the Dragon Emperor. But more than that, the meeting represented the end of 268 years of Manchu rule and a formal break in two thousand years of continuous imperial tradition.

* * *

The outcome of that fateful meeting was that Pu Yi abdicated on 12 February 1912. He had just entered his seventh year. Negotiations were conducted in his name by the Empress Dowager Jung Shu. His life and future role were agreed in what is known as the eight 'Articles of Favourable Treatment'. They stated that he would maintain his title and dignity and be accorded by the Republic of China 'the courtesies which it is customary to accord to foreign monarchs'. He was to inherit the personal fortune of the Ch'ing Dynasty and be funded by the state. Article three prescribed that he would be allowed to remain in the Forbidden City with his personal bodyguard and palace guards who would become members of the Republican Army.

The Articles ensured that the mausolea of the Manchus in Manchuria and the province of Chihli, in which Peking is situated, and the associated imperial temples of the family spirits would be maintained and that military guards for their safety would be provided by the republic. All current work on the mausolea would be completed at the expense of the republic. A further article assured the employment tenure of those who worked within the Forbidden City but there would be no further additions to the staff of eunuchs.[9]

Over the next two years various documents clarified the Eight Articles and extended security of privileges and titles to the Manchu princes. In effect Pu Yi's life remained unaltered and was still directed by the *Nei Wu Fu* ('Imperial Household Department') with its six hundred retainers and corrupt bureaucracy. Sun Yat-sen, with some reluctance, resigned his provisional presidency of the new republic at Nanking in favour of Yuan Shih-k'ai.

Pu Yi now lived a dual life: a mixture of childhood play and the tedious formality of court ritual. And in this land of curiosities and enigmas, from the spring months of 1912 to the snows of 1924 the emperor and the president both lived in the heart of the capital. For hours Pu Yi was expected to sit above his courtiers in the Dragon Throne and listen to interminable speeches on the day-to-day running of his household. The papers he stamped with the Imperial Seal were of no state relevance, but referred to domestic matters. As spiritual leader Pu Yi was expected to play a part in the rituals of ancestor worship of his Manchu imperial forebears.

It was a world of make-believe. Pu Yi's tutors daily reminded him of his position and that one day he might be restored to the throne. In this he was encouraged by his Chief Tutor, the Confucian scholar Chen Pao-shen, the self-proclaimed 'Political Director to the Emperor'. A passionate royalist, Chen fervently believed that the republic would fall and his pupil would be restored; to this end he constantly bombarded his seven-year-old charge with his conservative views.

Outside the Forbidden City Yuan Shih-k'ai was still president of the republic, but he treated Pu Yi with great respect. Even Yuan's civil servants and staff were allowed to wear the elaborate court dress when visiting the young emperor on state business. And when the Empress Dowager Jung Shu died in 1912, President Yuan ordered state mourning. Tutor Chen and the pro-restoration supporters saw this as a change of mood significantly in favour of Pu Yi's restoration. Their fervour blinkered them from reality and the machinations of the wily Yuan.

All the clues were there. The Presidential Palace, opposite the Forbidden City, was now sumptuously embellished. Army bands began to serenade the president at mealtimes and he took on an imperial mien. Members of Pu Yi's staff began to keep an hourly vigil, watching what happened at the Presidential Palace, and gossip abounded that Yuan wanted to be emperor himself. For a while Yuan had toyed with the idea of restoring Pu Yi, but during 1915 he organized a plebiscite and engineered matters so that he himself was proclaimed emperor.

Yuan's reign lasted only a few weeks. Opposition to him grew and skirmishes broke out with enemy cadres and his own loyal troops. Yuan achieved a spectacular *volte-face*, declared himself President of the Republic only, and averred that he was a loyal supporter of the republic and wished only to serve the people. By June 1916 he was dead.

The news of Yuan's death spread rapidly through the Forbidden City and Pu Yi's staff were euphoric. By 1917 a restoration attempt was made for the eleven-year-old emperor by General Chang Hsun (1854–1923), Viceroy of Kiangsu Province. As controller of the vital Tientsin area from his base at Hsuchow on the Tientsin–Peking railway, General Chang Hsun, dubbed the 'pig-tailed general',[10] was granted an audience with Pu Yi, through Tutor Chen, now elevated to the position of Grand Guardian. They met in the Hall of Mental Cultivation. Well tutored in how to conduct the interview, Pu Yi was puzzled by the exchange of banalities in the audience. Two weeks later the general returned to the Forbidden City to 'restore' Pu Yi with 'a mandate from the people'.

Events now proceeded rapidly. Pu Yi signed new imperial edicts of restoration with a Regency Board including Tutor Chen and the general; to Pu Yi's dismay his father was not included. President Li Yuan-hung, who as Vice-President had succeeded Yuan Shih-k'ai, fled to Peking's Legation Quarter and the city celebrated the return of the emperor.

Pu Yi remembered this episode vividly:

> Ch'ing clothes that had not been seen for years reappeared on the streets . . . Shops did a booming trade . . . Tailors sold Ch'ing dragon flags as fast as they could make them . . . theatrical costumiers were crowded with people begging them to make false queues out of horsehair. I still remember how the Forbidden City was crowded with men wearing court robes with mandarin's buttons and peacock feathers in their hats.[11]

Peking was largely a pro-monarchist society, but elsewhere support for the restoration was thin. General Chang Hsun lacked the qualities of an emperor-maker, and he was regarded with mistrust by the powerful army commanders. During the short restoration period the Forbidden City was bombed: three small bombs dropped from a small plane piloted by a republican officer. The event caused more panic than destruction and General Chang Hsun sought refuge in the Dutch Legation. Pu Yi's restoration had lasted twelve days and he abdicated for the second time on 20 July 1917. The decree of abdication was never published, for in assuring the exoneration of Pu Yi, Grand Tutor Hsu Shi-ch'ang wrote a document reporting that the emperor 'returned sovereign power to [*the people of China*]'.

Republican China's authorities were lenient. General Chang Hsun was allowed to go into honourable retirement within the British Concession at Tientsin with minimum punishment, and the Articles of Favourable Treatment which had previously allowed Pu Yi his privileged position in the Forbidden City were not amended. President Li Yuan-hung was disgraced and replaced by the conservative aristocrat Feng Kuo-chang.

Following this a new parliament convened and declared war on Germany. The act was a nod towards the pro-war monarchists and a derogatory gesture to Sun Yat-sen, who opposed any Chinese action in the First World War from his base at Canton, where he fulminated as commander-in-chief of a military government that was having little effect other than dividing northern and southern China. In addition, China's reparation payments from the previous wars were cancelled.

In all this Pu Yi's advisers forgot nothing and learned nothing. They continued to jockey for the restoration of the emperor against a politico-military background which was to bring ruin to China. Japan was strengthening her hold of former Chinese assets and territory and was virtually in economic control of Manchuria. Although China's support of the allies in the First World War was minimal – they supplied a labour corps in France – yet they believed that their support would win them allied assistance to thwart Japan. The Treaty of Versailles of 28 June 1919 soon dissuaded the Chinese on that score as former German concessions in China were confirmed to the Japanese. From their very different places in history Emperor Pu Yi and Reginald Fleming Johnston stepped on to the international stage, to be part of each other's lives for years to come.

CHAPTER 4

IMPERIAL TUTOR: SECRETS OF THE PURPLE PALACE

In 1918, when Pu Yi was twelve, the new President of the Republic Hsu Shih-ch'ang and those nearest the Dragon Throne debated whether 'elements of a western education' should be included in Emperor Pu Yi's instruction. Those involved in the discussions included Johnston's acquaintance the diplomat Li Ching-mai, former Chinese Minister at the Court of Franz Joseph I, Emperor of Austria and King of Hungary, at Vienna, who had fled to Weiheiwei in the turmoil of 1911. The first proposal was that the position of foreign tutor should be given to an American diplomat and educationalist who had followed a distinguished career in China; however, he was soon to become the US Chargé d'Affaires. Next on the list was Reginald Fleming Johnston.

Through Li Ching-mai's influence with President Hsu Shih-ch'ang and the Imperial Court, Johnston was offered the position at the end of November 1918, although his candidature was not wholly acceptable to the more reactionary members of the Imperial Court. They believed that he would make the emperor 'too modern'. However, a compromise was reached and Johnston was employed solely as 'English Language Tutor'. The Envoy Extraordinary and Minister Plenipotentiary to the Court at Peking, Sir John Newell Jordan (1852–1925) handled the formal offer of the tutorship through the Colonial and Foreign Office in London for approval and Johnston was seconded to Peking from Weiheiwei in early 1919.

Johnston was to remain a Colonial Office employee – at his own request, as it assured him some security of tenure. His contract with the Imperial Court was confirmed to cover the years 1919–22, wherein he was to tutor for three hours per day and have two months annual leave.[1] His salary of £500 as a Colonial Office employee[2] was now supplemented by a generous emolument from the Imperial Court, plus regular cash and artefact gifts from the emperor.[3] In *Twilight in the Forbidden City* Johnston notes:

> On the eve of each of the great festivals it was customary for [the emperor] to send presents of money, for which we gave formal thanks (*hsieh En*) at the audiences in the Palace of Cloudless Heaven. Other gifts, of porcelain, books, pictures, jade and other things from the imperial collections, were also occasionally presented by the emperor in person, merely as tokens of goodwill. Sometimes presents of fruit and cakes came also from the imperial dowagers . . . the arrival of gift-bearing messengers from the palace often caused a commotion in the neighbourhood.[4]

Gifts of ginseng (for throat conditions) were looked upon as an 'exceptional favour' from the imperial clan. Johnston also had a rent-free mansion which he furnished in traditional Chinese style.

Johnston prepared a memorandum of his arrival at Peking and his first meeting with the boy emperor Pu Yi for the Colonial Office. This survives in his writings.[5]

> MEMORANDUM (7 March 1919)
> On arrival at Peking on 22 February 1919, I was met at the station by Mr Ni Wen-te, one of the President's secretaries. Two days later I was received by the emperor's father, Prince Ch'un (whom I had met many years ago at Hong Kong) and by Prince Tsai T'ao (another brother of the late Emperor Kuang-hsu), at their respective residences. The latter takes a special interest in the boy's education

and is generally regarded as the most enlightened and progressive of the Manchu princes. His reception of me was extremely cordial, and he has invited me to call upon him at any time when I wish to discuss matters connected with the boy's welfare. He entertained me at a dinner-party on 5 March, and on this occasion I was presented to several other members of the imperial family, including Prince Tsai-hsun, another of the young emperor's uncles.

On 27 February I paid an official visit to President Hsun Shih-ch'ang; and on that and following days I exchanged visits with the following officers connected with the Manchu Court: Shih Hsu, Comptroller of the Household and Grand Guardian; Ch'i Ling, a Manchu who is a relative of the emperor's mother, the Princess Ch'un; Shao Ying, a Minister of the Household; and the Imperial Tutors Liang Ting-fen, Chu I-fan and I-Ko-T'an. On the 8th inst. I am to be a guest of the officers of the Household and the Tutors at a dinner at the Wagons-Lit Hotel.

My formal introduction to the boy emperor took place on 3 March [a date fixed as auspicious by the court astrologers]. He was dressed for the occasion in court dress, and was attended by a number of functionaries in uniform. On being conducted into the audience-chamber I advanced towards the emperor and bowed three times. He then descended from his seat, walked up to me and shook hands in European fashion. He remained standing during the rest of this short interview and asked me a few conventional questions, mainly about my official career in China. [Pu Yi was apparently taken-aback when Johnston addressed him in fluent Chinese.] When the interview was over I withdrew to a waiting-room and was informed that the emperor wished to begin his English lessons immediately and would receive me again in a less formal manner as soon as he had changed his clothes. In the interval, I received visits from a large number of palace officials and eunuchs who offered congratulations on my appointment. On re-entering the imperial schoolroom in the Yu-ch'ing Palace, in which the formal reception had taken place, I found the emperor seated at a table on which were placed the books which I had already selected for him. He asked me to sit down at his side, and from that moment our relations have been those of teacher and pupil and have been quite free from formality.

The young emperor has no knowledge whatever of English or any other European language, but he seems anxious to learn and is mentally active. He is allowed to read the Chinese newspapers, and evidently takes an intelligent interest in the news of the day, especially in politics, both domestic and foreign. He has a good general knowledge of geography, and is interested in travel and exploration. He understands something of the present state of Europe and the results of the Great War, and seems to be free from false or exaggerated notions about the political position and relative importance of China. He appears to be physically robust and well developed for his age. He is a very 'human' boy, with vivacity, intelligence, and a keen sense of humour. Moreover, he has excellent manners and is entirely free from arrogance. This is rather remarkable in view of the extremely artificial nature of his surroundings and the pompous make-believe of the palace routine. He is treated by the court functionaries with all the outward reverence supposed to be due to the 'Son of Heaven', he never goes outside the 'Forbidden City' and he has no chance of associating with other boys except on rare occasions when his younger brother [Prince Pu Chieh] and two or three other youthful members of the imperial clan are allowed to pay him short visits. Even his daily visits to the schoolroom are made the occasion of a kind of state procession. He is carried there in a large chair draped in imperial yellow, and he is accompanied by a large retinue of attendants.

Although the emperor does not appear to have been spoiled, as yet, by the follies and futilities of his surroundings, I am afraid there is no hope that he will come unscathed through the moral dangers of the next few years of his life (necessarily very critical years for a

> boy in his early teens) unless he can be withdrawn from the influence of the hordes of eunuchs and other useless functionaries who are now almost his only associates. I am inclined to think that the best course to pursue in the boy's own interests would be to take him out of the unwholesome atmosphere of the 'Forbidden City' and send him to the Summer Palace. There it would be possible for him to live a much less artificial and much happier life than is possible under present conditions, and he would have ample space and opportunity there for physical exercise. It would be necessary, of course, to entrust him to the care of an entirely new set of servants and attendants who should be under the close supervision of some thoroughly trustworthy official specially selected by the president or any responsible member of the imperial clan who (like Prince Tsai T'ao) is fully acquainted with the circumstances and has the boy's welfare at heart. Perhaps I may find it possible, later on, to make some recommendations of this kind. At present it is, of course, too early for me to take any such action, though I have already, to some extent, made my views known to Mr Liu T'i-ch'ien (a relative of Lord Li and a friend of Prince Tsai T'ao's) and to Mr Ni Wen-te, the president's private secretary.

Thus Johnston described *inter alia* his first encounter with the boy emperor. But what would each actually have seen of the other? Johnston was a tall, blue-eyed, ruddy-complexioned, corpulent 45-year-old, with a shock of grey hair. To Pu Yi he was an elderly man. The boy emperor's experience of foreigners was limited; he had only seen foreigners in the flesh once before, when the Empress Dowager Jung Shu had entertained the wives of foreign diplomats. Pu Yi had found them with 'their strange clothes and their hair and eyes so many colours . . . both ugly and frightening'. In the pictures of foreigners which circulated in the Forbidden City in foreign magazines, which were smuggled into the Imperial Palace, Pu Yi observed 'they wore moustaches on their upper lips; there was always a straight line down the legs of their trousers; they invariably carried sticks'.[6] His eunuch attendants filled his impressionable mind with remarks that the foreign devils hung lanterns on their moustaches, never bent their legs and hit people with sticks to civilize them.[7]

Pu Yi averred in his *Journals* that Johnston's blue eyes and grey hair 'made me feel uneasy' but he was super-attentive to what his tutor said. Johnston had settled down as a conservative bachelor, who held strong beliefs in the rightness of the British Empire and its superior form of government over all others. After twenty years in China he believed that the country was not ripe for republicanism and that it would be best served by a British-style constitutional monarchy; its difference from an absolute monarchy he explained to Pu Yi. From day one Johnston was repelled by the myopic, venal Manchu Court, but his snobbishness made him enjoy his artificial status. He loved the right to enter the Forbidden City in a chair carried by two bearers. Only a few months into his new employment he was elevated to the second of the nine mandarin ranks of imperial honour and received the 'sable robe'. As time went by Johnston's unique position led courtiers of all ranks seeking the ear of the emperor to ask him to convey their requests to his young charge. Johnston tried to reform the ways of the court, but he was to prove no match for its corruption.

How did Pu Yi appear to Johnston? The new tutor found a gangling, awkward, short-sighted, timorous, absent-minded youth. Yet Pu Yi was capable of kindness, dignity and moral courage. Although he liked women and was not narrow-minded, Johnston was something of a sexual prude and became blinkered to Pu Yi's more venal faults. More than one biographical source has suggested that the emperor was bisexual.[8] He was certainly sadistic towards women, and violent in his punishment of attendants. Yet although he idealized – and even idolized to some extent – his imperial pupil, Johnston was always somewhat in awe of his pupil's royal status; as a conventional and rather staid Scotsman, he was unable to understand Pu Yi's tantrums and emotional life. Indeed, he never even referred to them in his writings.

Johnston's milieu until 1924 was to be the *Da Nei* ('Great Within') of the *Tze-chin-ch'eng* ('Purple Forbidden City'), the environs of which were sacrosanct; those entering without permission were liable to 'a hundred blows of the bamboo', or 'death by strangulation'.[9] Johnston became a daily visitor to the *Yang-Hsin Tien* ('Hall of the Nurture of the Mind'), and for the most part conducted his tutorials in the *Yu-ching Kung* ('Imperial Schoolroom'), between the *Chai Kung* ('Hall of Fasting') and the *Feng Hsien Tien* ('Chapel of the Imperial Ancestors') by the Ching Yun Gate.

Among the milling throng in the Forbidden City were the numerous *nu kuan* (ladies-in-waiting) and *kung nu* (maidservants) serving the four *t'ai fei* (dowager consorts), the *hu chun* (palace guards) and, the most curious of all for any westerner like Johnston, the thousand or so eunuchs. During his years of service Johnston was to make many enemies among these castrated careerists.

The cult of the Chinese *huan kuan* ('castrated man' – eunuch) was perhaps the most sordid and macabre of all political systems. Although there is an early reference to Chinese eunuchs in the *Tao Chuan* (Commentary of Tso)[10] for the year 535, historians generally agree that it was not until the reign of Han Huang Ti (146–67) that eunuch power began to make itself felt.

The instance of eunuchs at the Chinese court came about because, as they originated as servants of the court ladies, it was necessary 'to protect the chastity and purity of the ladies-in-waiting and other court ladies'.[11] As eunuchs were both guards and servants of the imperial concubines, they early became masters of intrigue in the hothouse of political and hierarchical jockeying that imbued the emperors' personal lives. Further, as Dr Jitsuzo Kuwabara pointed out:

> The Chinese have always been a very jealous people. This is easily understood from reading such books as the *Li Chi*, the Confucian scriptures, where rules of etiquette and manners are sensitively arranged so that there would be no imaginable chance of one being suspected of having illicit relations with the opposite sex. Under

> such circumstances, it may have been a matter of course for eunuchs to have been used as a means of avoiding the suspicion of immorality and soothing jealous minds in the Chinese society.[12]

Whatever the reason for castration, the system engendered a cadre of greed, duplicity and thirst for power which spawned corruption within the Imperial Court. The castrations were enacted outside the walls of the Forbidden City by practitioners who did nothing else, and for a few pence. The severed part, *pao* ('treasure'), was retained by the castratee as a kind of badge of rank, and was buried with him on death; without it he would not be a whole man and could therefore not dwell with his ancestors.

Johnston estimated that there were about a thousand eunuchs remaining in the court of Pu Yi in 1919, survivors of the three thousand or so who had inhabited the Forbidden City in the days of the Empress Dowager Tzu Hsi.[13] The others had disappeared with their largely ill-gotten gains to their homelands of Chihli and Shantung, or had scattered to monasteries and hermitages in the Western Hills and elsewhere. Those remaining were employed as personal assistants and chairbearers to the emperor and the remaining dowagers. More were overseers of palace buildings and the artefacts therein or were employed in menial tasks from kitchen hands to fire-watchers.

Eunuchs of the highest grade were the crimson-uniformed *yu-ch'ien t'ai chien* ('Eunuchs of the Presence'), who served the emperor alone, although technically they were employees of the *Nei Wu Fu*. Through the ages some eunuchs had risen to places of great power: the Empress Dowager Tzu Hsi's Chief Eunuch Li Lien-ying achieved the influence expected of a Viceroy.

From the age of three Pu Yi's constant companions were his eunuchs. He remembered their actions when he left his rooms:

> In front went a eunuch whose function was roughly that of a motor-horn; he walked twenty or thirty yards ahead of the party

> intoning the sound 'chir, chir', as a warning to anyone who might be waiting in the vicinity to go away at once. Next came two Chief Eunuchs advancing crabwise on either side of the path; ten paces behind them came the centre of the procession. If I was being carried in a chair there would be two junior eunuchs walking beside me to attend to my wants at any moment; if I was walking they would be supporting me. Next came a eunuch with a large silk canopy followed by a large group of eunuchs, some empty-handed, others holding all sorts of things: a seat in case I wanted to rest, changes of clothing, umbrellas and parasols.
>
> After these eunuchs of the Imperial Presence came eunuchs of the Imperial Tea Bureau with boxes of various kinds of cakes and delicacies . . . They were followed by eunuchs of the Imperial Dispensary . . . at the end of the procession came the eunuchs who carried commodes and chamberpots. If I was walking, a sedan-chair, open or covered according to the season, would bring up the rear. This motley procession of several dozen people would proceed in silence and order.[14]

Johnston noted that during 1919 and 1920 a eunuch was always present during his lessons with Pu Yi indicating, to his annoyance, that the *Nei Wu Fu* remained nervous about the *Wan-sui-Yeh* ('Lord of Ten Thousand Years') being in such close proximity to a foreign devil. Johnston's first real encounter with the graft system operated by the eunuchs occurred on the day of his formal introduction to the boy emperor, 3 March 1919. As he waited in the ante-room to be summoned to begin the first lesson, eunuchs swarmed round him, hissing their congratulations and demanding money on the 'auspicious occasion' as was the custom expected of all newly appointed courtiers. A canny Scotsman, Johnston bartered with them and demanded in return a receipt in exchange for the largesse [dubbed 'red-packet money']; the eunuchs, unwilling to put themselves on record as extracting money, sidled away. Johnston had made them his enemies for life. On one occasion, when he caught them operating a scam selling imperial artefacts for cash, they endeavoured to implicate Johnston by planting filched goods in his mansion. He faced them with their infamy and they backed off. Johnston worked to persuade the emperor to lessen the influence of the eunuchs, who dubbed the tutor the 'Old Foreign Buddha' behind his back.[15]

* * *

The position of Imperial Tutor was one of high rank at the Manchu Court. The venerated office of teacher in China was long set out in such works as the *Li Chi* ('Records of Rights and Ceremonies'), one of the five *Ching* classics:

> When a pupil meets his teacher on the road, he should hasten towards him and bow. If the teacher addresses him, he should give a fitting reply; if the teacher is silent, he should retire quickly . . . A pupil should wait upon his teacher and serve him without regard to mere conventions. As long as his teacher lives he must serve him zealously, and should pay him the tribute of sincere mourning for three years after his death . . . If a prince is anxious to civilize his people or make them courteous and well-bred, it is with the school that he must begin. Uncut jade cannot be turned into a serviceable vessel; if men are uneducated they do not know how to conduct themselves. Thus it was that the wise kings of old, when settling their states on sound foundations and in ruling their people, made education their primary care . . . It is from the teacher that the ruler learns the art of government; thus nothing should be a matter of graver concern than the selection of a teacher . . . There are two men in his realm whom the ruler cannot regard as his subjects. One is the man who in the ritual sacrifices to the dead personates the royal ancestors; the other is his teacher. That was a right and proper rule which ordained that when the teacher was addressing the Son

> of Heaven he should not face the north [in audience an emperor sat facing south and the subject stood facing north]. That was how honour was done to the office of teacher.[16]

Although he was unaware of it at the time, Johnston's appointment as *Ti Shih* ('Imperial Tutor') was resisted by the more traditional members of the emperor's court, but he was treated with courtesy by his pupil Pu Yi from the start. The emperor always rose when Johnston entered the room, and Johnston sat in a place of honour on Pu Yi's left, facing west as tradition prescribed. Once he realized that there were members of Pu Yi's court who resented his presence, Johnston, rather perversely, went out of his way to annoy their sensibilities.

Always proud of his position at court, Johnston flaunted the rank the emperor gave him in the mandarinate system. One biographer of Pu Yi, Brian Power, averred that Johnston was 'opinionated, supremely confident and pompous', and Pu Yi remembered:

> The Household Department rented a house for him in the city and he had it decorated as a court official would have done. Upon entering the gate one could see four red tablets on which were written in black ink:
> COMPANION OF THE YU CHING PALACE
> PRIVILEGED TO BE CARRIED IN A SEDAN CHAIR WITH TWO BEARERS
> AWARDED THE HAT BUTTON AND ROBES OF THE FIRST RANK
> ENDOWED WITH THE RIGHT TO WEAR A SABLE JACKET
> Whenever he received a special honour he would have a formal memorial written to thank me.

Pu Yi was also to recall: 'After he had received the hat button of the highest grade, he had a full set of court clothes and headgear made. He posed for a photo in these in front of his summer house in the Western Hills, and sent prints of it to his many friends and [selected] relatives.'[17]

Despite the honour of arriving at the palace in a two-bearer chair, Johnston often used his car or rode on horseback to his work at the Forbidden City, knowing full well that his modernity and idiosyncratic prominence made the traditional courtiers seethe behind their fans.

In 1919 Johnston was one of five imperial tutors to Pu Yi. The other four were Liang Ting-feng, who had formerly been Chief Justice of the Province of Hopei, and was now too old to attend the imperial court schoolroom; Ch'en Pao-shen, who progressed to be *T'ai Fu* ('Grand Tutor'); Chu I-fan, who was a distinguished educationalist who combined imperial tutorship with the role of physician-in-ordinary to His Majesty; and I-Ko-T'an, who was the only Manchu tutor. The three tutors who regularly attended the schoolroom alongside Johnston tutored Pu Yi one after another, according to rank, from around 6 am to 11 am before Johnston's own stint. Way back in 1911 the Imperial Astrologer had divined that the most auspicious time for Pu Yi to study was between 7 am and 9 am, but the divination gave no indication that this was the daily peak time of Pu Yi's intellectual powers as he inattentively thumbed through the *Thirteen Classics* (the fundamental texts of Confucianism) placed for his edification. He was more interested in the huge 7ft high chiming clock with arms as long as his own.

Johnston made his first entry into the Forbidden City to tutor the boy on 3 March 1919, and as he crossed the threshold of the *Shen Wu Men* ('The Gateway of Spiritual Valour') he stepped from the new republican China of the twentieth century into a monarchy that was already ancient when Romulus founded Rome on the Palatine Hill in 753 BC. Here, too, the passage of time was calculated in the old way: the lunar calendar set the days which marked the occasion as the Eleventh Year of Hsuan-T'ung (the boy emperor's reign name).

From the modern crowds of bustling Peking, Johnston merged with the palanquins of colourfully robed mandarins and high court officials, and the jingling horses of ceremonially gowned noblemen and court chamberlains. At every door stood attendants waiting to hand down the great from their conveyances while eunuchs clad in the livery of their class hovered to fulfil ceremonial roles.

Johnston sent detailed letters about his life at court to his old friend Stewart Lockhart, explaining court procedure as he learned it and his role within its complicated nuances. The letters express his pride, honour and delight in his part in it all.[18] At the heart of the Forbidden City the boy emperor Pu Yi worked through the daily ceremonies based on centuries-old court rites, as he fidgeted in the ceremonial robes that gave him so much discomfort. All was overseen by the corrupt *Nei Wu Fu* whose tentacles took in the Forbidden City, the imperial mausolea and the *Yuan Ming Yuan* (Summer Palace). The *Nei Wu Fu* was headed by the comptroller, the *Tsung Kuan Nei Wu Fu Ta-ch'en*. In 1919 this position was held by Shih-Hsu (d. 1922). During his time at the Imperial Court Johnston was the only foreigner granted the honour of observing and playing a role in the great court rituals.

Arriving at the Forbidden City around 1.30 pm each day, Johnston interspersed his English language lessons with informal chats about current affairs. He had been warned that Pu Yi's mind had a *fou* ('floating') quality and was often inattentive; the stimulus of intellectual variety was Johnston's attempted cure. Lessons were conducted in Chinese as Pu Yi's progress with spoken English was slow.

In his first hours of tutorship Johnston was dismayed to find that the only English language teaching aids were a few copies of Lewis Carroll's *Alice's Adventures in Wonderland*, published in 1865. Clearly this was inadequate and Johnston began to introduce volumes of his own choosing as well as newspapers and magazines from Britain. Slowly he acquainted Pu Yi with the rudiments of world history in general and British history in particular. To this were added discussions on philosophy, Scotland, the strengths (in Johnston's opinion) of the imperial system of government and the tutor's prejudices on what he saw as the 'dangers' of growing American influence in China through the missionaries he so despised. It was all topped off with Johnston's reservations about democracy.

As they flicked through articles on international affairs, Pu Yi began to realize that Johnston's 'teaching me English was not so important in Johnston's eyes as training me to be the English gentleman he was always talking about'. The 'gentrification' of Pu Yi was also carried on when the young emperor was entertained by Johnston at his mansion nearby; here British table manners were expounded and behaviour in British society explained. The rituals of English afternoon tea were introduced wherein the repast was defined not as a mollifier of hunger but as a raising of the flagging spirit. Tea was no longer to be slurped, or a postprandial belch to resound across the table, even though in Chinese polite society this was a compliment to the host's cuisine. Knives and forks were practised with, table settings arranged and small talk indulged in.[19] (Ironically Johnston used chopsticks when he dined alone, or with friends at dinner parties at his mansion.)

Pu Yi became fascinated by Johnston's clothes. The steel-grey suit and waistcoat, the white-starched collar, the dark-blue tie figured with white crowns, the trouser creases you could almost cut paper with, and the highly polished leather shoes whose heels made a sharp metallic click as pupil and tutor walked the thoroughfares of the Forbidden City.

Slowly Pu Yi developed pro-Western tastes, and ordered Western clothes; Johnston cringed at the style of garment courtiers had procured from theatrical costumiers in the city and the baggy size too large for the emperor's thin frame. Pu Yi came in for a severe admonition on the clothes' unsuitability. They made him look a fool, which angered Johnston greatly. Western furniture and artefacts were also acquired for use daily by Pu Yi who could not learn enough about Western ways. As his English language studies progressed Pu Yi requested that Johnston give him an 'English name'. It was his intention to use this name when he signed letters in English, memos for Johnston or other Europeans, or photographs. Johnston came up with a list of names of the kings of England and Pu Yi chose Henry for himself, dubbing his brother Prince Pu Chieh William and selecting other royal names for other siblings.

Lessons were well settled into their routine by 1920 when Johnston considered that Pu Yi's educational progress would be greatly enhanced if he had a companion to study alongside. Johnston selected Pu Yi's cousin Prince P'u-Chia (nicknamed Arthur in Pu Yi's English scheme), son of Prince Tsai-T'ao. The court rivalry between Prince Ch'un and Prince Tsai-T'ao caused some friction but Johnston's suggestion was accepted and an amicable arrangement of *pan-tu* (companion-readers) was organized, with Prince Pu Chieh also joining the lessons.

All the time Pu Yi was sizing up his tutor whom he regarded as 'the major part of my soul':

> I thought that everything about Johnston was 'first-class' and even went so far as to regard the smell of moth-balls that always came from his clothes as fragrant. He made me feel that Westerners were the most intelligent and civilized people in the world and I thought him the most kind and learned. I do not think that even he realized how deep an influence he was having on me. The beautiful woollen cloth of his suits made me doubt the value of all the silks and satins in China and the gold fountain-pen in his pocket actually made me ashamed of writing with brushes; his cream note-paper I thought far finer than our hand-made Chinese paper . . . [Johnston remarked on the fineness of the emperor's calligraphy when he was writing English.]
>
> Once he arranged for a British military band to come to the palace and play for us. I was so excited I almost cried and thereafter considered Chinese music hardly worth listening to, even the ancient and stately ceremonial music seemed far less majestic . . . Once Johnston remarked that the English word for the Chinese queues was 'pig-tails'; I was horrified and shocked and within the hour had cut mine off![20]

The boy emperor's bold hair cutting – he had to do it himself as no one at court would even consider such sacrilege – caused hysteria among the dowager aunts, but his act caused thousands to do the same;

meanwhile the more traditional members of the court shook their pig-tailed heads that again the English tutor was going too far.

Johnston was concerned that life in the Forbidden City was 'detrimental to [the emperor's] health, physical, intellectual and moral'.[21] He pressed for Pu Yi to be allowed to visit the Summer Palace more regularly, but visits were to prove rare. Believing, too, that the young emperor had little useful exercise – he was carried everywhere in palanquins and sedan chairs – Johnston introduced the first bicycle to the Forbidden City. Delighted with this new form of mobility, Pu Yi ordered bicycles for Prince Pu Chieh and a few of his attendants. Johnston's next innovations were to be even more expansive.

One 'revolution' the conservative courtiers noted with particular dismay was the installation of telephones. Johnstone encouraged their proliferation in the Forbidden City, little realizing that his pupil would take every opportunity to contact him as his enthusiasm for the 'foreign contraption' grew. Pu Yi had also ordered a fleet of cars for the Forbidden City by 1921 and with Johnston's encouragement he persuaded the security department to agree to his first official drive through the streets of Peking. All such innovations were opposed every step of the way by the *Nei Wu Fu*.

Johnston also came into conflict with the imperial authorities over Pu Yi's eyesight. It was clear to him that the boy emperor was short-sighted and needed glasses. The dowager consorts vehemently opposed the suggestion that a foreign oculist should be consulted. The imperial eyes were both precious and sacred. It was out of the question, thundered the most influential of the dowagers Tuan K'ang, to submit the Son of Heaven to the ministrations of a foreign devil. But Pu Yi's eyestrain was causing headaches, bad temper and inattention. So Johnston pressed Prince Ch'un on the matter, threatening to resign if nothing was done. Permission was eventually granted and Johnston wrote to Professor H.J. Howard, head of the department of ophthalmology at the Peking University Medical College. Howard paid a visit to the Forbidden City and Pu Yi was prescribed suitable spectacles. Dowager Consort Tuan

Sir Reginald Fleming Johnston KCMG, CBE, tutor to the last Emperor of China from 1919 to 1925, pictured in academic dress. Johnston was a Professor of Chinese Studies at the University of London from 1931 to 1937. (School of Oriental and African Studies, University of London)

Goshen Bank House, Canaan Lane, Morningside, Edinburgh, where Reginald Fleming Johnston was born in 1874. (Charles J. Smith)

Falcon Hall School, Morningside, Edinburgh, shortly after its opening in 1889. Reginald Fleming Johnston attended the school as a day boy and left in 1890 to enter his father's law office. The statues to the left and right of the front door are of the Duke of Wellington and Lord Nelson. The building was demolished in 1909. (Royal Commission on the Ancient and Historical Monuments of Scotland)

Interior of the walled city of Weiheiwei, viewed from the Huan-Ts'ui-Lou Tower, c. 1908. In the distance can be seen the island of Liukung, the harbour and the European settlement of Port Edward. (Reginald Fleming Johnston, Lion and Dragon in Northern China*)*

Reginald Fleming Johnston with the Commissioner's dog Tommie and attendants at the shrine on Quork's Peak, Mount Macdonald, c. 1908. (Fleet Surgeon C.M. Beadnell RN)

Above: Commissioner of Weiheiwei Sir James H. Stewart Lockhart, with the priest and attendants at the temple in the military district of Ch'eng Shan. (Reginald Fleming Johnston, Lion and Dragon in Northern China*)*

Alice Walter, Reginald Fleming Johnston's 'dream woman', aged around twenty, soon after she came to Weiheiwei in 1911. (The Estate of M.I. Johnston)

The Great Watergate, Peking, with the peasants' market and food booths, pictured around the turn of the century. This was a popular haunt of Johnston's on his bicycle trips. (China Research Fund)

Companies of Royal Navy personnel, led by warrant officers, were sent to defend the British concessions and legations in China in time of disturbance. British consular offices did not have consular police. In due course Johnston encouraged their commanding officers to meet his imperial pupil. (China Research Fund)

Above: The 124th Baluchistan Infantry pipe the Royal Inniskilling Fusiliers, 24 October 1911. Such regiments were present to protect British interests as China fragmented in the year of Pu Yi's deposition. (China Research Fund)

Prince Ch'un, brother of Emperor Kuang Hsu and father of Pu Yi, was appointed regent on behalf of his son in 1908. The infant Emperor Pu Yi stands on the right, with his brother Pu Chieh (b. 1907) seated on their father's knee. (China Research Fund)

Tsai-feng, His Imperial Highness Prince Ch'un (d. 1951), the mediocre and vacillating father of Emperor Pu Yi. He disowned his son for perceived pro-Japanese activities. (China Research Fund)

內務府信牋

敬啟者現由奏事處傳出奉

旨

賞莊　於十四十五十六日在

漱芳齋聽戲等因欽此用特布達專此即頌

公綏

內務府啟

In honour of the imperial wedding certain members of the Nei T'ing *(Inner Court) were invited to special Command Theatre Performances. This is Johnston's invitation. It reads:*

'Communication from the imperial household department. It is respectfully intimated to you that the Office of Memorials to the Throne has passed to this department an Edict from His Imperial Majesty saying:

'The honour of attendance at the Lodge of Fresh Fragrance [the Palace Theatre] on the 14th, 15th and 16th days [of the lunar calendar] is hereby conferred upon Chuang [Johnston]. Such is His Imperial Majesty's pleasure.

'This is transmitted to you for your special information. May peace be with you.'

Hung shang *(His Imperial Majesty) Aisin Gioro Pu Yi (1906–67), by-named Emperor Hsuan-T'ung, Son of Heaven, Lord of Ten Thousand Years, last Manchu Emperor of China, aged around two. (China Research Fund)*

The Empress Dowager Tzu Hsi, whose corrupt and xenophobic rule of the vast, crumbling Manchu Empire brought the nation to bankruptcy and anarchy. Two days before her death she declared Pu Yi her successor. (China Research Fund)

The Empress Dowager Tzu Hsi and selected ladies of her court, photographed in 1903. The infant Pu Yi owed his position to her influence. Behind the empress stand the daughters of the former Minister to the Chinese Legation at Paris, Yu-Keng, and his wife. To the left is 'Radiant Concubine', second wife of Emperor Kuang Hsu, and to the right is Tzu Hsi's niece the Empress Consort Lung Yi. (China Research Fund)

Prince Ch'un's household. Pu Yi's mother stands on the left. (China Research Fund)

Emperor Pu Yi: large numbers of such formal pictures were given to visiting international dignitaries. (China Research Fund)

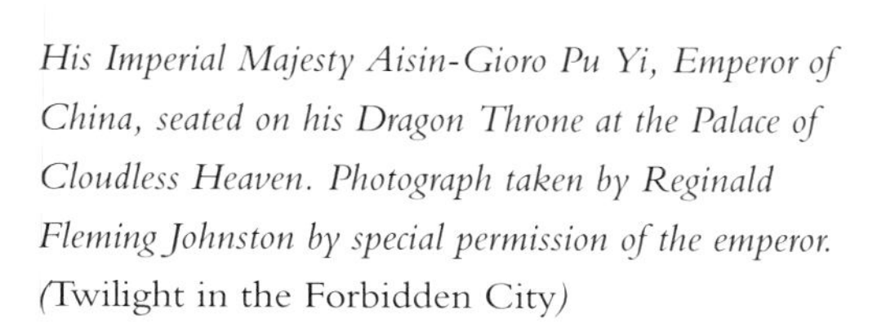

*His Imperial Majesty Aisin-Gioro Pu Yi, Emperor of China, seated on his Dragon Throne at the Palace of Cloudless Heaven. Photograph taken by Reginald Fleming Johnston by special permission of the emperor. (*Twilight in the Forbidden City*)*

Pei-Ling, the tomb of T'ai-Tsung, second Manchu Emperor of China, who ruled from 1626 to 1643. When Pu Yi assumed the Dragon Throne he automatically became guardian of all the tombs of his Manchu ancestors. In July 1928 the Manchu tombs were blown open and robbed by Chinese soldiers to Pu Yi's great distress, as one of his sacred duties as emperor was their protection. (China Research Fund)

*The garden and covered walkway at Johnston's quarters at the Summer Palace. Print from a photograph taken by Johnston. (*Twilight in the Forbidden City*)*

Prince Ch'ing, Chief Grand Councillor and the last Manchu Prime Minister (1903–11). He was the quintessential courtier of the old school encountered by Reginald Fleming Johnston. (China Research Fund)

The Manchu General Yuan Shih-K'ai, President of the Chinese Republic for a few months, with his staff. He forced the abdication of the Manchu regents and was known as the 'traitor general'. He died in 1916. (China Research Fund)

Eileen Edna Le Poer Power, later Mrs Michael Moissey Postan. This photograph was taken during her trip to China, funded by the Albert Kahn Travelling Fellowship, in 1920–21. At the time she was Director of Studies in History at Girton College, Cambridge. On this trip she met Johnston for the first time. (Lady Cynthia Postan)

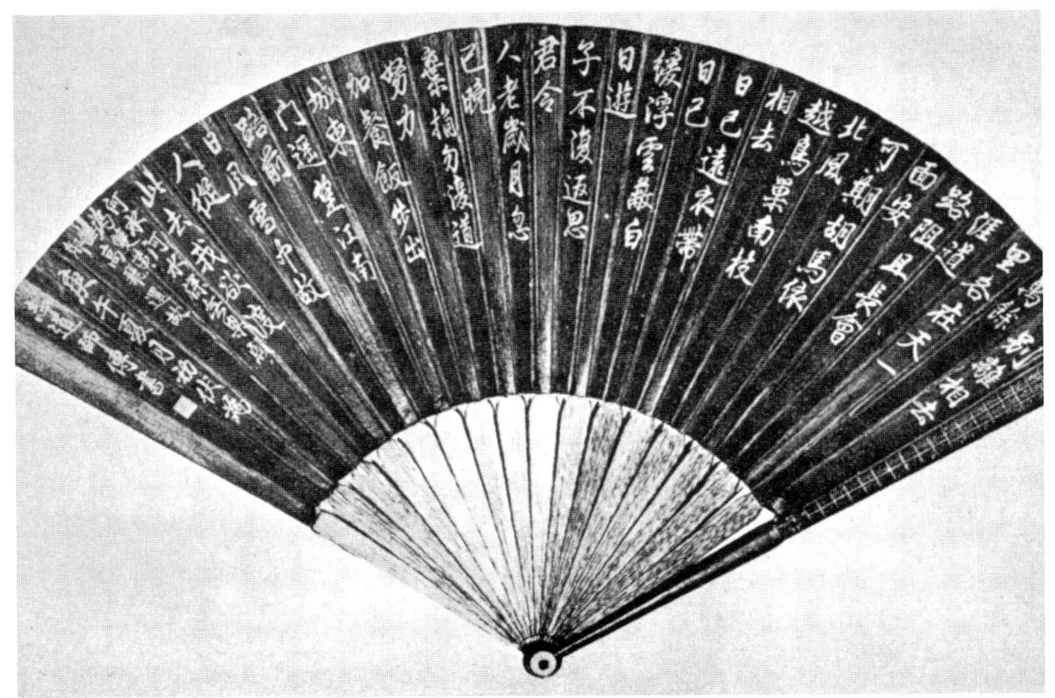

*This fan was given to Reginald Fleming Johnston by the Emperor Pu Yi as a farewell gift at their parting on 15 September 1930. Johnston averred that the emperor had personally inscribed the calligraphy of the Chinese poem of farewell. (*Twilight in the Forbidden City*)*

Emperor Hirohito of Japan reviews his troops while riding his famous imperial grey horse. The Japanese were to play key roles in Emperor Pu Yi's life. (Japan Research Projects)

His Imperial Majesty Pu Yi, Emperor of Manchuria. He is shown here dressed in the state uniform as Commander-in-Chief of the Japanese puppet state of Manchuquo, 1935–45. (Japan Research Projects)

Above: The former Emperor of China Pu Yi, now the Japanese puppet Emperor of Manchuquo, on a visit with his staff to the Japanese Ministry in Hsingking, the new capital of Manchuquo. With him walks the Japanese minister and his deputies, flanked and saluted by members of the Imperial Japanese Army. (China Research Fund)

Reginald Fleming Johnston, second from right, with Emperor Pu Yi and Major-General Francis Arthur Sutton, ex-Royal Engineers, who was then mining in Korea. (Hulton)

In 1934 Reginald Fleming Johnston purchased the rugged island of Eilean Righ, part of the Portalloch Estate, Kilmartin, West Argyllshire. He transformed the island in Loch Craignish into a 'tiny piece of China'; a pavilion-style house set amid acres of poppies modelled on a Chinese poppy garden was its centrepiece. (Author's Collection)

The main house and subsidiary buildings of Sir Reginald Fleming Johnston's home at Eilean Righ, photographed in the late 1980s. Near the house Johnston flew the yellow flag of the Manchus and drawn up on the foreshore were little boats painted in imperial yellow. (Author's Collection)

K'ang was not informed about the glasses until Pu Yi had been wearing them for some time. Johnston noted that, as she had not actually forbidden Howard's visit,[22] her ritual suicide in protest had been avoided.

Pu Yi's intellectual curiosity was further stimulated by Johnston in a number of ways. He invited officials from the British Legation, as well as the admirals and generals visiting the Legation, to call on him. He held meetings for Chinese writers and poets at the Forbidden City, but these were not wholly a success as a visit by any Chinese to the Imperial Court circle was deemed 'a political act, and an automatic endorsement of the pro-monarchical establishment'.[23]

For some time Pu Yi had been taking an increased interest in the British royal family and the possibility of foreign travel for himself. When Johnston announced that HRH Edward, Prince of Wales, had also been at his old alma mater of Magdalen College during 1912–14, Pu Yi embarked on a kind of hero worship. Johnston did not enlighten the young emperor that all academic aspects of Magdalen had been a bore to the Prince of Wales who was more interested in the college's point-to-point meets. Pu Yi studied all the papers reporting the Prince of Wales's activities with great interest, particularly his 'extraordinary interest in clothes'. On one occasion, his emulation of the Prince of Wales resulted in an explosion of temper from Johnston. Pu Yi recalled the event in his *Journal*: '[After a reception for foreign guests] I returned to the Mind Nurture Palace and took off my dragon robe and changed into a Chinese long gown on top of which I put on a Western-style jacket. Also I put a peaked tweed cap on my head.'

Johnston came in with some foreign guests; the tutor's face turned red and the guests gave the emperor strange looks. What had he done wrong? Later, when the guests had gone, Pu Yi was still puzzled about Johnston's fury, and asked its cause. 'What kind of style is that?' Johnston asked furiously. 'Your Majesty the Emperor – for the Emperor of China to wear a hunting cap! Good God!'

Nevertheless Pu Yi continued to shape his daily routine to what the Prince of Wales's taste might be, as reflected in the magazines from

England, and he became greatly excited at the news that the Prince of Wales had set out on the *Renown*, on 26 October 1921, for a trip to the Far East. After tours of India and Burma, and en route for Japan, the Prince of Wales arrived at Hong Kong where he was met by the Governor Sir Reginald Stubbs. As a 'monarch in exile', Pu Yi was not represented at the Hong Kong celebrations, much to his disappointment; his dismay was to be deepened when he learned that the Prince of Wales would not be journeying to Peking. He asked Johnston to acquire for him a signed photograph of the Prince of Wales.[24]

Pu Yi talked of travelling to Britain and perhaps taking up studies there. Should this happen, Johnston expressed his hope that the emperor would go to Magdalen College. The President of Magdalen, Sir Herbert Warren, was keen on the idea when Johnston broached the subject. Johnston knew that Pu Yi's spoken English was not good enough for ordinary membership of the university or college, but it was thought possible that Pu Yi and his entourage could rent a property at Oxford so that he might spend a year attending classes.

Through the diplomatic grapevine Johnston heard that King George V was interested in the fact that Pu Yi had a British tutor and followed the young emperor's activities. In the British Legation it was thought that the king would welcome a visit by Pu Yi and that the Foreign Office would not put up any formal objection. In the short term, though, such a visit would not be possible because of China's political position.[25]

All of the innovations encouraged and introduced by Johnston were making the young emperor restless. His growing disaffection with his cloistered existence alarmed the dowager consorts who feared that he would soon take steps to escape from his 'gilded prison', thus breaking up the traditions that secured their positions and livelihood. Something had to be done to take his mind off such things. They came up with the answer: a marriage must be promptly arranged.

CHAPTER 5

THE RESTLESS DRAGON: MARRIAGE AND FLIGHT

In the years following his appointment as Imperial Tutor, Reginald Fleming Johnston had found a soulmate in his fellow tutor Ch'en Pao-shen. Their joint love of mountains took them, despite Ch'en's age, on many expeditions to the Western Hills. To Johnston this was his shangri-la, and through the generosity of President Hsu Shih-ch'ang, he acquired a dwelling in the vicinity which he dubbed Cherry Glen.[1] It was a small estate some five hours' ride from Peking near the village of Ying T'ao Kou. Here Johnston escaped from the hothouse incarceration of the Forbidden City to ramble and ride over the hills, seeking peace and quiet for his writing and steadily reading through his accumulation of ten thousand volumes in Chinese and English.

Always a generous host, Johnston would regularly welcome guests from Peking and passing diplomatic staff and travellers to Cherry Glen, yet he valued his solitude. Writing to Sir Herbert Warren[2] he described Cherry Glen as having a 'romantic ravine', mountain streams with 'delicious' bathing-pools, and an attractive Chinese-style dwelling; nearby was a temple, seven small summer-houses and a whole variety of seasonally changing scenes to delight his spirit. Here, he averred, he would like to spend the rest of his life. But there were always pressing demands urging him to return to Peking.

Because of the cloistered, restrictive and reclusive nature of Emperor Pu Yi's existence, he was hardly at liberty to pursue the opposite sex with a view to matrimony or indeed anything else. Even if he had wanted to select his own female companionship, the choice of suitable girls for an emperor was limited. In any case, even though he was now sixteen, the subject of romantic or sexual dalliance was not high on Pu Yi's list of priorities as he vegetated in the Forbidden City. Yet marriage must be contemplated, insisted the Dowager Consorts, so a whole range of suitable young females outside Pu Yi's immediate orbit were selected by the Dowagers, his father Prince Ch'un and several other functionaries; after much arguing they formed a short list of four potential spouses for Pu Yi.

In later years he was to write:

> To me the girls seemed much the same and their bodies looked as shapeless as tubes in the dresses. Their faces were very small in the pictures and I couldn't see whether they were beauties or not . . . It did not occur to me at the time that this was one of the great events of my life, but I had no standards to guide me. I casually drew a circle on a pretty picture.[3]

Pu Yi had chosen Wen Hsui, a plump, plain thirteen-year-old from an aristocratic Manchu family. Rumour had it that she had been added to the list as a makeweight. The Dowager Consorts began to twitter that Wen Hsiu was unsuitable as empress material. Yet they nodded to the idea that she could become a *shu-fei* ('secondary consort' – a euphemism for a concubine) should Pu Yi wish it. The emperor must choose again, added the message.

This time Pu Yi's pen circled the photograph of a sixteen-year-old English-speaking girl, Kuo Chia; named by future historians the Lady Wan Jung, she was the daughter of Jung Yuan, a rich and influential scion of a Manchurian family. Wan Jung had been educated at Tientsin at an American missionary school. This time the Dowager Consorts signalled their approval, hinting that Pu Yi might have all the others on his list as his 'secondary concubines'. No, he declared; enough was enough.

Pu Yi did not meet his bride until their wedding day, which was the climax of a programme of traditional rituals and processions. Johnston took great delight in cataloguing the marriage events at some length.[4] It all began on 11 March 1922 with an announcement in the *Court Gazette*: 'Jung-yuan chih nu Kuo Chia shih li wei huang-hou' [Kuo Chia, daughter of Jung Yuan, is hereby created empress]. This rather bald statement was in accord with Chinese tradition; as stated by the Chinese Imperial Law the prospective bride had to be elevated to imperial rank before the nuptials took place.

On 17 March Wan Jung was transported to Peking by special train. Here she was ceremonially greeted by court functionaries, republican representatives and a guard of cavalry. She was conveyed with due pomp to the *Hou Ti* (Mansion of the Empress), outside the Forbidden City and within the old Tartar City, to follow a course of training in the etiquette of the court. On 6 April Pu Yi went in solemn pilgrimage to the shrine of his Manchu ancestors to inform them of his marriage.

In the background there was increasing political tension as a number of independent groups plotted the official restoration of Pu Yi. Each group had its own agenda and spied on the rest. Among them, and perhaps the most significant, was the Manchu warlord Chang Tso-lin (1875–1928) whose agents penetrated the Forbidden City. There was talk of escalating civil war and Johnston kept a packed suitcase at the emperor's quarters in case he had to flee. Johnston further elicited from the British Minister at Peking, Sir Beilby Alston, an agreement that in case of danger to the emperor's person he might bring him to the British Legation. However, the risk of a clash between Chang Tso-lin and another pro-monarchist warlord, Wu Pei-fu, faded and thoughts were focused on an equally pressing need.

In early June Johnston became alarmed. Pu Yi was having second thoughts about his marriage. He told his brother Pu Chieh that he wanted to go to England, to study at Oxford like Johnston. With the help of his brother, Pu Yi gathered a number of choice pieces of imperial treasure and had them converted into money, secreting the resulting hoard at Tientsin, for his proposed trip. To further his plans, Pu Yi then approached Johnston for help.

On 3 June Johnston received a confidential message from Pu Yi asking him to go to the palace at 3 pm, and take two cars to the Tung-hua Gate. Johnston did so; he drove his own Ford and hired another car with a driver from a public garage. Then Pu Yi called Johnston into his office at the Yang-Hsin Tien and, making sure that they were not overheard, told Johnston that he wanted him to drive him, his luggage and several trusted attendants to the British Legation. Once at the Legation Pu Yi proposed to draft a telegram to 'the people of China' giving up his position as 'idle pensioner of the State' and renouncing his imperial title and privileges. Then he would make plans for a trip to Europe and, he hoped, a course of study at Oxford.

Johnston was taken by surprise. Thinking quickly, he offered three reasons why the emperor should change his mind. The previous day, Johnston reminded him, President Hsu Shih-ch'ang had resigned, and the press and public, as well as international representatives of the main powers, would assume that they 'had been engaged in political intrigue together'. Moreover, if an international incident was sparked off by the flight, Sir Beilby Alston would be unable to offer him refuge at the British Legation. And – most unconvincingly to observers in hindsight – the emperor would be accused of renouncing his position, pension and titles to 'save face', by giving up voluntarily that which was to be taken away from him anyway (the latter was certainly not the case). Besides, Johnston reasoned with the distraught Pu Yi, in the absence of a president or parliament, there was no one in China to accept or acknowledge his renunciations.

Johnston's report of the events in his *Twilight in the Forbidden City* avers that Pu Yi had been motivated by 'growing disgust with the corruption which he knows is rife throughout the palace'.[5] However, during an interview with Pu Yi's brother Pu Chieh several decades later, writer Edward Behr, then researching his book *The Last Emperor*, was told that Pu Yi 'had wanted desperately to break out of his palace to try to start a normal life'.[6]

Of Johnston's own motivation in refusing to help Pu Yi, Charles Moore made this comment: 'I heard from [name deleted] at HMG Legation at the Imperial Palace that Reggie was in a funk concerning the little emperor's wishing to defect like that. He was afraid that somehow he would be castigated by the [Colonial Office, London] for encouraging the boy to skip to London. Certainly there would have been a great fuss, as HMG were not much interested in [Pu Yi] anyway . . . Then there was the possibility of Reggie losing his billet.'[7] Moore was expressing the local Legation gossip that Johnston loved his position as Imperial Tutor and mandarin far too much to jeopardize his future at the Imperial Palace by backing any escape plans. Thwarted, Pu Yi reluctantly settled down to the preparations for his marriage.

As the astrologers plotted each propitious day for events the marriage programme charts were slowly worked through by the *Ta Hun Li Ta Ch'en*, the four imperial commissioners of the wedding arrangements, Prince Tsai-T'ao, Imperial Tutor Chu I-fan, Minister of the Household Shao-Ying, and his colleague Ch'i Ling. On 21 October 1922 the Presents of Betrothal were taken to the bride. The presents' procession made a bizarre skein of guards, musicians, courtiers and cavalry winding through Peking's byways to the Mansion of the Empress. On *lung-t'ing* (dragon pavilions – rather like sedan chairs) forty pieces of satin and eighty rolls of cloth were borne amid gifts of two saddled horses and eighteen sheep. This was but the token dowry of Manchu tradition for the lavish gifts of porcelain, gold and silver, and presents for the bride's parents were yet to come. Already the prospective father-in-law Jung Yuan had been given imperial rank and made Minister of the Presence.

Two weeks later, on 12 November, the *Ta Cheng Li* (Marriage Contract Rites) were enacted, with more gifts for the bride and her parents. Even the bride's household servants were given cash awards on this occasion. The last of the three main ceremonies preliminary to the marriage were performed on 30 November, with the 'Rites of the Golden Seal and Scroll'; the latter being the most important symbolic imperial distinction from the emperor to his bride. On the same day the *shu-fei* Wen Hsiu entered the palace as a prospective bride, in readiness to lead the court ladies who would soon welcome the empress-bride.

Johnston would remember the marriage day all his life. It began at around 3 am with the assembly of a huge marriage procession at the Mansion of the Empress. According to Manchu wedding rites everything had to take place at night. The early morning hours of 1 December 1922 were crisp and clear as the procession of sixty lantern bearers, seventy flag bearers, umbrella carriers, guards, republican infantry, cavalry, courtiers and brass bands playing European and Chinese music, set out for the Forbidden City. The light of the almost full moon glinted on weapons and musical instruments as the specially bedecked ceremonial sedan chair carrying the bride rocked on the shoulders of twenty-two bearers on its way to the 'Great Within'. As the carts loaded with the bride's trousseau and the imperial officers carrying the yellow pavilions containing such symbols as the 'Golden Seal and Scroll' passed by, the crowd-lined streets fell silent in awe and curiosity.

The chair bearing Wan Jung, Johnston noted, was the *feng-yu* bridal seat that Westerners dubbed the 'Phoenix Chair' after the Chinese mythical bird called the *feng*. The chair was covered in scarlet silk and *feng-huang* symbols for happiness and prosperity for the bride; this would be Wan Jung's special symbolism hereafter to complement her husband's five-clawed dragon, the *lung*.

On arrival at the gates of the Forbidden City, the bearers put down the Phoenix Chair; they were replaced by eunuchs who would carry her alone to her new life. Inside the *K'un-Ning Kung* (Palace of Earthly Peace), Pu Yi awaited his bride on his Dragon Throne. Wan Jung descended from the Phoenix Chair and processed into the palace, and then sank to her knees in *kowtow* before her husband as the Imperial Decree legitimizing their marriage was intoned by a court official. The wedding ceremony was completed with the shared drinking from the Nuptial Cup and partaking of the wedding feast set out on the Dragon Phoenix Couch.

Recollecting the occasion years later for his ghosted *Journal* Pu Yi commented:

> I felt stifled. The bride sat on the bed, her head bent down. I looked around me and saw everything was red; red bed curtains, red pillows, a red dress, a red skirt, red flowers, and a red face . . . it all looked like a melted wax candle. I did not know whether to stand or sit; [I] decided that I preferred the *Yang-Hsin Tien*, and went back there . . . How did Wan Jung feel, abandoned in the bridal chamber? What was Wen Hsiu, not yet fourteen, thinking? These questions never even occurred to me.

In the *Journal* he later confided: 'I thought if there had been no revolution I would now be starting to rule with full powers. I must recover my ancestral heritage.' However, this hardly squares with his trying to persuade Johnston to help him escape to Europe a few brief months previously.

Strange to tell, this reference to Wan Jung – to whom Pu Yi gave the name of Elizabeth – was almost the only mention of her in his *Journal* of 1964; about Wen Hsiu there is no comment at all. This has been interpreted by later biographers of the emperor as proof of 'sexual inadequacy'. One of them, Edward Behr, pursued the matter for his book *The Last Emperor*.[8]

Behr observed that no one at court could break protocol in order to give Pu Yi a sex education, least of all Johnston with his Presbyterian background. The fact that Pu Yi left his wife (and his concubine) on their wedding night, said Behr, would certainly suggest that Pu Yi was 'impotent, extraordinarily immature sexually, or already aware of his homosexual tendencies'. In an interview with the emperor's brother Pu Chieh, Behr asked why Pu Yi had never had any children? Pu Chieh replied that the ex-Emperor was found to be 'biologically incapable of reproduction'. Certainly as the months went by after the wedding and their honeymoon romps around the Forbidden City on their bicycles lost their attraction, Wan Jung was increasingly left alone in her own quarters by Pu Yi to brood; she became more moody and bored.

The series of court ceremonies continued in the days after the wedding. On 3 December, for the very first time, the emperor and his new empress held an informal reception for two hundred distinguished foreigners; this was at Johnston's discreet suggestion. Johnston was given the honour of being one of those who introduced the foreigners to the imperial couple. Rehearsed by Johnston, the emperor addressed the foreigners in English: 'It is a great pleasure to us to see here today so many distinguished visitors from all parts of the world. We thank you for coming, and we wish you all health and prosperity.' He then toasted the company in champagne.[9] Delighted, the foreign guests burst out with spontaneous applause, and on leaving they were given cloisonné artefacts and silver trinkets as mementos of the occasion.

In the wedding Honours Johnston was promoted from the second to the highest of the official mandarin grades – *t'ou pin ting tai*. In his heart he was now 'truly Chinese' and a 'Scottish mandarin'.[10]

* * *

Despite the excitements and anxieties of the imperial wedding, thoughts of flight from his 'prison' at the Forbidden City were never far from Pu Yi's mind. He knew that most people around him opposed any such move: Johnston prevaricated over any trip to Britain; the monarchists did not want him to be absent from his Dragon Throne in case a chance of restoration arose; and the hangers-on wanted him to stay in order to secure their livelihoods. There were also logistic difficulties in planning such a flight as the eyes and ears of the *Nei Wu*

Fu were everywhere. Pu Yi realized that the 'Articles of Favourable Treatment' would not remain in place indefinitely. His unsettled frame of mind caused him to reveal his thoughts for flight to his brother Prince Pu Chieh. Together they conspired to flee. The cache of money that they had already stashed away at the safe house at Tientsin was further supplemented to pay for the escape.

During Saturday 24 February 1923 Johnston attended a reception hosted by the new President of the Republic Li Yuan-hung. At the reception he was approached by the wife of W.J. Oudendijk, the Dutch Foreign Minister, who said that a slight indisposition had kept her husband at their Legation, but he was anxious to meet with Johnston at the soonest possible moment. Excusing himself from the reception, Johnston went immediately to the Dutch Legation where Oudendijk told him that Pu Chieh had recently informed him about the emperor's planned escape, with the intention of going to the British Legation at Tientsin. Pu Yi had asked for the minister's assistance to escape and to accompany him to Tientsin. Did Johnston know of the plan? No, he did not, he affirmed.

In *Twilight in the Forbidden City* Johnston explains that he decided to do nothing to assist or dissuade Pu Yi in what he thought was an understandable but rash scheme. The Dutch Minister had agreed in the meantime to receive Pu Yi at the Dutch Legation and to accompany him to Tientsin; he would not take part in the actual escape plans, lest his actions cause embarrassment to his government, but he reserved a private compartment on the night train to Tientsin in preparation. As Oudendijk talked to Pu Yi on the telephone to discuss the final arrangements for the emperor's reception at his Legation the line went dead.

A short while later Johnston was summoned to the Forbidden City and was immediately shown in to Pu Yi's private apartments. The emperor explained to Johnston what his plan had been and how it had been betrayed to his father by a eunuch attendant. An almost hysterical Prince Ch'un had ordered the surveillance of Pu Yi to be strengthened and to shoot the emperor if necessary if he tried to escape. Representatives of the *Nei Wu Fu* and the Republican Government interviewed Johnston about the incident, fully convinced that he was behind the plan. Despite Johnston's assurances of his innocence he was not believed.[11]

The incident slowly blew over and the turgid life of the Forbidden City went on. As the emperor had grown up, Reginald Fleming Johnston undertook fewer tutorial duties and became more of an unofficial adviser to the court.[12] Indeed, a year later, Johnston's duties within his tutorial remit became so slight that he offered to resign; the emperor was appalled and refused to agree to such a move.[13]

One aspect of Pu Yi's court life which concerned Johnston was the gradual disappearance of imperial treasures. The Republican Government's subsidy (equivalent to around one million pounds in modern values) was woefully inadequate to sustain court expenses, corruption and graft. The ineffective Regent, Prince Ch'un, had presided over expensive events, and the imperial treasures had dwindled to pay bills and line pockets. Johnston was horrified that no inventory of the treasures existed. He thus urged Pu Yi to become more interested in his imperial inheritance, which included artefacts from the palaces at Mukden and Jehol.

Alas, Johnston's concern came too late – the Manchu (Ch'ing) Dynasty was fast approaching bankruptcy. Nevertheless in early June 1923 Pu Yi ordered an inventory to be taken of the *Chien Fu Kung* (Palace of Established Happiness) where a large accumulation of antiques – including 2,685 gold statues of Buddha – and other treasures were kept. Terrible events intervened on 26 June: fire swept through the palace and reduced the building and its contents to ashes.

Had fate really struck? There was a strong rumour that the court functionaries and eunuchs, who had been conducting what Pu Yi called an 'orgy of looting' over the years, had set fire to the palace in order to cover their pilfering. Although arrests were made, no culprits were ever brought to justice. Forced to act, on 14 July Pu Yi expelled the eunuchs from the Forbidden City. Many eunuchs believed that their expulsion, accelerated by the arrival of troops of the Republican Army, had been on Johnston's advice. He received a variety of death threats and pleas for him to intercede with the emperor. Only when the Dowager Consorts wailed that they had no servants left did Pu Yi allow a total of fifty eunuchs to return. When the eunuchs had departed parts of the Forbidden City were closed and the whole 'took on a desolate abandoned air', said Pu Yi. On the site of the Hall of Supreme Harmony, Johnston set out a tennis court, which Pu Yi also used as a cycle stadium.[14]

* * *

Emperor Pu Yi's position had always been tenuous as the 'Articles of Favourable Treatment' offered him only 'temporary' lodgement at the Forbidden City. Johnston now advised his young friend to think about decamping to the *Yuan Ming Yuan* (Summer Palace). In China as a whole growing left-wing bias was developing in intellectual and political movements and Johnston believed that it was only a matter of time before the weak Republican Government fell.

The *Nei Wu Fu* were not enamoured of the suggested move. They blustered that the Summer Palace was too small to house Pu Yi and his entourage in proper style, but the real reason for their disaffection was that such a move would mean the sacking of hundreds of hangers-on who were bleeding the imperial funds. Finally, however, Johnston's arguments of economy, comfort, safety and convenience won favour with Pu Yi who moved the scheme forward by making two important appointments in early 1924.

Pu Yi appointed his senior tutor and adviser, the Confucian scholar Cheng Hsiao-hsu (d. 1935) to oversee reforms of the reluctant *Nei Wu Fu*; adding insult to injury to this recalcitrant body he made Johnston *Pan shih ta ch'en* (Commissioner in Charge) of the Summer Palace, with the task of getting it ready for Pu Yi's transfer. Johnston was given personal quarters in the *Chi Ch'ing Hsien* (Pavilion of Clearing Skies), an annex of the *Hsieh Ch'u Yuan* (Garden of Harmonious Delight).

Amid an atmosphere of sniping and petty complaints from the *Nei Wu Fu* officials, Johnston set about his task with great enthusiasm. His plan was to make the Summer Palace self-sufficient. He even suggested opening a portion of the palace to paying visitors, not only selling tickets but fish from the lake and even licensing traders within the complex and establishing hotels. Although the Summer Palace had been allowed to fall into disrepair, not too much needed doing and, pushing aside inflated contractors' estimates via the *Nei Wu Fu*, he proposed to deal directly with the Peking craftsmen.

Meanwhile Cheng Hsiao-hsu was making little headway with the layers of on-the-make employees at the Forbidden City. He managed to pare down some employment lists, but the head of the Household Bureau, Shao Ying, proved too skilled an operator of palace staff non-cooperation. Discouraged, Cheng Hsiao-hsu resigned, pleading ill-health, after three months in his appointment, greatly upset that Pu Yi's father Prince Ch'un too had been working against him.

After a short trip to his retreat at Cherry Glen, Johnston returned to the Summer Palace on 21 October 1924 to be told that one of the Dowager Consorts, Tuan K'ang, the last consort of Emperor Te Tsung, had died. The next day he drove back to Peking, noticing nothing untoward. But in the early hours of 23 October an agitated servant told Johnston that troops were sealing off sections of the old Tartar City and that people were seeking places of safety.

Believing that another local mutiny of troops had broken out, Johnston was not greatly perturbed, but he began to feel less confident when the telephone lines were cut. He made his way to the Forbidden City, observing subtle changes from the norm as he went. There was increased martial activity: soldiers in strange uniform – not that of the imperial bodyguard – were guarding public buildings, and there were rumours that the president, Ts'ao K'un, who had replaced Li Yuan-hung on the latter's resignation, was under house arrest.

Slowly Johnston pieced together what had happened. The on-going power struggle between the warlords Chang Tso-lin and Wu Pei-fu had escalated. The curiously named 'Christian General' Feng Yu-hsiang (1880–1948) had thrown in his lot with Wu Pei-fu, but had now swung his army south with the intention of taking Peking. As the general opposed special treatment for the imperial family and was known to be ambitious to rule himself, Johnston realized that his imperial pupil was in danger.

On arrival at the Forbidden City, Johnston sought out the emperor who awaited him in his study. Together they observed the troop movements beyond the city walls for a while, then took lunch. As Prince Ch'un and others arrived to discuss matters with the emperor, Johnston left to trawl the usual sources of gossip and information in Peking, such as the Grand Hotel des Wagon-Lits, the Peking Club and the foreign Legations.

By 2 November General Feng's troops had completely sealed off the Forbidden City, but Johnston was allowed to come and go around his old haunts. He helped take away documents and 'articles of great value' for the emperor to deposit in the 'Honkers and Shankers' (the Hong Kong and Shanghai Bank). This done, Johnston returned to the Forbidden City and was shown a basket full of precious stones by the emperor which had belonged to the recently deceased Dowager Consort: 'they would have been stolen if they had been left in the palace' explained the emperor. He prompted Johnston to choose a keepsake and the tutor recalled that he chose a 'piece of exquisite green jade'.[15]

Visiting the Forbidden City once more on 3 November, Johnston found the place almost deserted, the staff in hiding or flown. Those left were largely concerned with the funeral ceremonies for Tuan K'ang. The next day Johnston returned to discuss the escape plans for the emperor and empress devised by Ch'eng Hsiao-hsu. Johnston's role was to smuggle the disguised imperial couple out of the Forbidden City in his Ford the following day. Alas, General Feng's soldiers arrived first.

The telephone lines having been restored, Johnston received an agitated call on 5 November from one of Pu Yi's uncles, Prince Tsai-T'ao. General Feng had completely surrounded the Forbidden City and access to it was now almost impossible. Johnston and Prince Tsai-T'ao together made an attempt to enter, but on the direct orders of General Feng's aide Lu Chung-lin they were turned away. Johnston did not know at that time that Pu Yi had already been taken from the Forbidden City under escort, and was now in the *Pei Fu* (Northern Mansion), his father's house. Pu Yi had been forced to sign the 'Revision of the Articles of Favourable Treatment', and had been reduced to the status of private citizen. While the emperor was obliged to cooperate with General Feng's phoney 'cabinet decisions', the remaining Dowager Consorts were threatening to take an overdose of opium if they were forcibly removed from the Forbidden City. Before he was taken away, Pu Yi had managed to negotiate their remaining in their lodgings on a temporary basis.

While Pu Yi gloomily contemplated his none-too-secure future his father Prince Ch'un was predictably undergoing a hysterical prostration. Later Pu Yi was to write:

> The storm . . . dropped me at the crossroads. Three roads stretched out before me. One was to do what the revised Articles suggested: to abandon the imperial title and my old ambitions and become an enormously wealthy and landed 'common citizen'. Another was to try to get the help of my sympathizers to restore the old Articles, to regain my title and to return to the palace to continue to live my old life. The third possible course was the most tortuous: first to go abroad, and then to return to the Forbidden City as it had been in 1911. In the words of the time, this course was 'using foreign power to plan a restoration'.[16]

There was a fourth way which Pu Yi left unmentioned – Johnston's 'dream goal' to have him go to Britain to become 'a genuine Oxford-educated Anglo-Chinese aristocrat'.[17]

Johnston made for the *Pei Fu* in his own car and to his surprise he was allowed to drive in. Soon he was admitted to the reception room where Pu Yi sat surrounded by Manchu officials. Pu Yi was eager to hear Johnston's news. At the tutor's prompting, that morning the Dutch Minister Oudendijk, the British Minister Sir Ronald Macleay and the Japanese minister K. Yoshizawa had gone to the new Foreign Minister, Dr C.T. Wang, to ascertain what would happen to the emperor and seek assurances for his safety. Dr Wang, with studied insult, emphasized that the former *huang-shang* (His Majesty) was now *Pu Yi hsien-shang* – 'Mr Pu Yi, a free citizen of the republic'. The 'Revision' document that Pu Yi had signed, Wang reiterated, secured the former emperor and his family's private property, allowed access to and protection of the imperial tombs, reduced the annual subsidy, but stripped Pu Yi of his titles and banished him from the Forbidden City. Yet in all that Wang said there was no stated guarantee of Pu Yi's safety and in the long term Johnston feared the worst.

From 5 November Johnston's house was under police surveillance with all Chinese visitors being turned away. The new regime resented Johnston's promotion of diplomatic intervention in seeking to protect the emperor; they had wanted the outside world to believe that Pu Yi had resigned voluntarily.

On 23 November 1924, a short while after Pu Yi had been ejected from the Forbidden City, the warlord Chang Tso-lin entered Peking and, with a small bodyguard of troops, forced out his ally General Feng. In his place he installed Marshal Tuan Chi-jiu as *Chih Cheng* (Chief Executive). Following this, restrictions of access to the emperor were removed and Johnston was told that he could visit his pupil once again. So Johnston recommenced his daily visits. Soon too, Chang Tso-lin sent word that he wished to see Johnston.

Johnston arrived at Chang Tso-lin's quarters bearing gifts from Pu Yi: a signed photograph of the emperor, and a topaz and diamond ring. Chang nodded gratefully over the photograph which he kept, but returned the ring. In flowery language he told Johnston that he had summoned him to take back assurances of safety to the emperor, and to discuss ways of setting in motion events that could achieve the restoration of the 'Articles of Favourable Treatment'.

Although this news seemed splendid, when Johnston reported back to Pu Yi the emperor was not convinced of Chang's good intentions. China was in a state of great upheaval, warlords were pursuing their own agendas and nothing seemed safe from sacrifice towards political ends. Johnston conferred with the emperor's advisers and agreed that Pu Yi should be moved as soon as possible to a safe haven close to the Legation Quarter. Johnston's opinion was that the emperor should be taken to the Legation Quarter 'and place himself under the protection of the foreign ministers'.[18] When this advice was relayed to Pu Yi he agreed to cooperate. Johnston added:

> I stressed the extreme importance of not saying a word about our plans to any one else in the *Pei Fu*, not even to the empress or to his father. The empress could follow later. If she accompanied us, her presence in the car would certainly attract attention and we might be stopped.

The emperor's escape from the *Pei Fu* was a mixture of deception, desperation and a Keystone Cops-type pursuit. Leading the way for the emperor, Ch'en Pao-shen and a house-boy, Johnston proceeded on the morning of 29 November 1924 through the halls of the *Pei Fu* to the car waiting in the courtyard. Just as they were about to slam the doors, Prince Ch'un's senior steward Chang Wen-chih, who had just been ordered to seek out Pu Yi and keep a close watch on him, insisted that he join their 'short drive'. Not wishing to create an air of alarm, Johnston agreed.

Unhurriedly the car passed safely through the police guard at the gate, but two armed officers jumped on to the running-boards. Johnston had planned their route through Peking to avoid Feng Yu-hsiang's troops, but he now came up with a ruse to get rid of the steward. With the two policemen still holding on to the car Johnston ordered the driver to accelerate through the maze of streets to the booths where they would stop to shop. The car pulled in at Johnston's instruction at Herr Hartung's photography shop, and he went in with the emperor to thumb through the display of photographic prints for sale.

A slip of the tongue caused Johnston to address Pu Yi as *huang shang*, causing the shop assistants to scuttle out in gossipy consternation, and by the time they left the shop a small crowd had gathered to view the emperor. As people silently stood and gawped at the living god that they had never before seen, Johnston and Pu Yi got back into the car. They had been unable to throw off the steward. Johnston now suggested that they go to the German Hospital near the foreign legations to visit his friend Dr Dipper. Pu Yi agreed. In a brief exchange with Dr Dipper on their arrival, Johnston explained their mission and that he would like to leave the emperor in the doctor's care for a while while he went to the foreign legations to secure a safe haven for his pupil. At this point, the steward seemed to have seen enough and returned to the *Pei Fu* to inform his master of what was going on.

The Dutch and Japanese ministers were both out, and so Johnston approached Sir Robert Macleay, the British Minister. He played down his own part in the escape to avoid any reprimand for his actions, and listened patiently while the minister intoned the official line that HMG could not be seen to be interfering in Chinese internal politics. Johnston explained that the Japanese Minister had already indicated that he would shelter Pu Yi. Macleay voiced no objection to such a move, which Johnston took as tacit approval, underlined by the minister's agreement that Johnston could move his lodgings to the British Legation to be near Pu Yi.

Johnston now went to the Japanese Legation and formally requested that Pu Yi be given a safe haven there. Japanese Minister Yoshizawa agreed after some diplomatically phrased hesitation and Johnston returned to the hospital to find Pu Yi gone. Alarmed, Johnston hurried back to the Japanese Legation. In the scramble to claim Pu Yi, the Japanese Legation's head of security, *Taisa* Takemoto, had pre-empted his minister and collected Pu Yi in a horse-drawn carriage. Afraid that they would be executed for allowing Pu Yi to escape, the two policemen who had jumped on to the running-boards and had clung on as the car sped through the Peking streets were granted asylum as Pu Yi's staff.

Unwittingly, Johnston had led his pupil into a danger that the speed of events and the necessity for fast thinking had caused him to overlook. Pu Yi's escape to the Japanese Legation caused a great sensation and the left-wing press ran a plethora of inaccurate reporting of events castigating Johnston for his part. He had expected this, but had not realized that the negative reports were based on information supplied to the press by the *Nei Wu Fu* which was anxious to implicate Johnston in the 'unlawful incidents'.

Soon Prince Ch'un arrived at the Japanese Legation with a bevy of Manchu officials. He begged, blustered and pleaded that Pu Yi should return, emphasizing that his son would be far safer with true Chinese friends. Comfortably ensconced in the Japanese Minister's state rooms, Pu Yi listened politely to his father but declined to go back.

By this time the empress was afraid that Pu Yi had deserted both her and his 'secondary consort'. At Johnston's suggestion, Japanese Minister Yoshizawa arranged for a diplomatic aide to go to the *Pei Fu* to rescue her. Despite much difficulty he succeeded. These actions enhanced Johnston's predilections towards the Japanese. Yet despite his great knowledge of the oriental mind, he still seemed curiously detached from the far-reaching consequences of his actions.

CHAPTER 6

THE SCOTTISH MANDARIN: SUCCOUR FROM THE RISING SUN

That Reginald Fleming Johnston delivered his esteemed pupil, the erstwhile Son of Heaven, into the hands of the Japanese is one of the ironies of the Johnston/Pu Yi story. It is difficult to understand Johnston's thinking concerning the Japanese. When he published his *Twilight in the Forbidden City* in 1934, Japan had already brutalized large numbers of Johnston's beloved Chinese, raped Manchuria, and had set in motion events that would end in the killing fields of the Second World War. Even so, Johnston apparently regarded the Japanese as able to give his pupil the best future opportunity as the puppet emperor of the territory of Manchuria, renamed *Manchuquo*. This would not happen for years but Johnston's actions could not have worked out better for the Japanese; he handed them an enormous propaganda *coup*.

Johnston knew the Japanese well. He had met them at Weiheiwei and in the diplomatic compounds of Peking, where at cosy after-dinner chats at the British Legation they had impressed him with their reserve, politeness and determination; many people in the international consulates believed that an influential role for Japan in China would help to combat the perceived Bolshevik menace from the north.

Johnston loathed Bolshevism and had criticized the British Foreign Office for not taking a firmer line against what he saw as rapacious

Russian interests in the Far East, particularly their support for the warlord Feng Yu-hsiang and their policies in Manchuria. Britain, however, having already had her fingers burned in Siberia in 1918 when, as a member of an international force, her troops had fought the Bolsheviks, was playing a non-confrontational role.

Johnston had made a special study of the Japanese stamping grounds in China. In letters to *The Times* correspondent in China, Dr George Ernest Morrison, for instance, he had noted that the Japanese had infiltrated deep into Asia, as far as the court of the Dalai Lama,[1] and he made a special journey to Tientsin in 1915 to study what the Japanese were doing.[2] Further, he had been privy to all relevant Colonial Office papers and reports on the Japanese from the Russo-Japanese War of 1904–5 onwards.

Japan's determination to secure a sphere of influence in China had been there for all to see from their seizure of the German concessions in Shantung in 1914. Any diplomat with any political awareness could see on all levels – whether military, with the Sino-Japanese Joint Defence Military Agreement, or commercial, with the huge Japanese investment in trade and railways – what was happening. These alone indicated Japan's massive and ruthless ambition in China. Moreover, it was clear that the Japanese Secret Service had infiltrated the Forbidden City. Yet in his skewed way of looking at Chinese affairs, Johnston had no real qualms about guiding Pu Yi into the maw of the Rising Sun.

Pu Yi now took up residence at the Japanese Legation. A complex of small buildings, it offered much less space than the *Pei Fu*. On his arrival Pu Yi was given a three-roomed apartment usually occupied by the Japanese minister Kenkichi Yoshizawa and his wife. This was a temporary measure, for soon Pu Yi's wife arrived, together with the young courtesan Wen Hsui, and the accommodation then proved too small. Instead, the Japanese gave them one of the legation houses inside the compound to use as living areas and as office space. Yoshizawa and his staff looked on in amusement as Pu Yi's wife and concubine squabbled loudly about who was to occupy which rooms, the mêlée spilling out into the legation compound as Pu Yi's bad-mannered retinue jockeyed for position.

Daily Pu Yi's father exhorted his son to return to the *Pei Fu*, and his old adviser Cheng Hsiao-hsu emphasized the mistake that Pu Yi was making by putting himself in debt to the Japanese. By this time Pu Yi held his father in some contempt because of the cowardice he had displayed during his son's adversity, and largely because of this he refused repeatedly to go back to the *Pei Fu*.

Pu Yi remained at the Japanese Legation from 29 November 1924 to 23 February 1925. During this time he did not leave the Legation Quarter but was a regular visitor to Johnston at the British Legation. They particularly enjoyed their evening walks together on the short portion of the ancient city wall of Peking that formed the southern boundary of the Legation Quarter. This was outside Chinese control, and from the high walls they could see the wooded parkland surrounding the Altar of Heaven. Although not within sight, the white marble construction was a symbol of all Pu Yi had lost. Once it had been the holiest place in China, where the emperor stood, as father and petitioner for his people, personally to address and commune with the gods. The yellow tiled roofs of the Forbidden City gleamed in the setting sun and reduced Pu Yi to tears. He sank his head in sorrow on to Johnston's chest, and as his old friend soothed him a lone dark figure was seen coming towards them in the encroaching darkness. The nervous Pu Yi feared assassination, but Johnston recognized the figure as Karakhan, the Soviet ambassador. Pu Yi remembered the incident years later and recalled how he and Johnston had returned to the British Legation and a private dinner together.[3]

Outside the compound both Pu Yi and Johnston were being increasingly vilified by such groups as the *Fan Ch'ing T'ung Meng* (Anti-Manchu League), which began to put pressure on the British Minister Sir Ronald Macleay to have Johnston recalled, or for the Republican government to have Johnston expelled. Their mouthpiece on one occasion was the Chinese newspaper *Min Pao*, whose rantings were translated in the English press on 11 August 1925:

> Ever since the arrival of the former emperor in Tientsin, Mr Johnston has been making overtures to all the ministers and consuls of the European imperialist countries in China in the name of his pupil. He did his best to win their support in a restoration movement by offering various concessions. As a result of his intrigue, the British *chargé d'affaires* [C.M. Palairet] has come under his influence. Since the Shanghai outrage of May 30 [At a demonstration the crowd were fired on by British police and nine students were killed; a strike followed where four more demonstrators were shot by British police. A boycott of British goods was set in motion and several anti-British demonstrations took place in such places as Peking and Canton] Mr Johnston has been taking a more prominent part in this monarchical plot together with the British chargé.[4]

To his fellow colonial officers, Johnston's behaviour had become more and more bizarre and he was dubbed a 'scandalmonger and meddler'. In the British watering-holes in the Legation Quarter he was criticized for his 'viceregal manner'. Yet to help them curb the propaganda excesses of the Anti-Manchu press, the Republican Government requested that Johnston should make a formal public reply. This Johnston did in the *Peking and Tientsin Times* on 12 August:

> Even in his retirement in Tientsin, the nineteen-year-old emperor is not free from the bitter and unchivalrous attacks of his enemies. Not content with having deprived him by force of his rights and privileges accorded to him in the original abdication pact, they are now attempting by every possible means to deprive him of such privileges as remain to him under the revised pact imposed upon him at the time of the *coup d'état* last November. Charges are

> incessantly being made against him of intriguing for a monarchist restoration. In this morning's Chinese press, for example, it is stated that he is surrounded at Tientsin by active members of the monarchist party; that he has established close relations with the various foreign consuls in Tientsin; that he has recently applied to a certain foreign Power for protection, and has promised *when restored to the Throne* to grant that Power various valuable privileges in China; and that he is allying himself with a certain military party, also with a view to a monarchist restoration. It is hardly necessary to say that not the smallest fragment of evidence is produced to support these wild assertions.[5]

All the anti-monarchist groups looked upon Johnston with suspicion. At best he was a foreign devil on the make, at worst a spy (although on whose behalf he was spying remained uncertain as *all* foreign residents in China were thought to be spies for their own countries). Others believed that Johnston's affiliations were located further east. Yet in fact Johnston was already regarded with equal suspicion by the Japanese. After the Japanese had vanquished the Chinese in the Sino-Japanese War, the *Joho-kikan* (military intelligence department) of the *Dai Nippon Teikoku Rikugun* (Imperial Japanese Army) had opened files on people they considered dangerous to their plans for China. Pro-Chinese Westerners were high on the list, with Johnston among them.

The Japanese knew a great deal about Johnston and they had noted his many trips to the Chinese hinterland. Were his many 'surveys' a part of a British espionage plan to thwart them? Their agents in the Forbidden City had already reported Johnston's 'dream' of taking Pu Yi to Europe. They could not be sure of Johnston's intentions but *Chusa* (Lieutenant-Colonel) Kenji Doihara, former head of special espionage missions in eastern Siberia and North China, ordered that a special watch be kept on him.

Kenji Doihara, a graduate of the *Rikugun Shikan Gakko* (Army Academy) class of 1904 and the Army War College in 1912, became one of Japan's most prominent 'China hands'. In 1931, as Director of the Military Intelligence Bureau at Mukden, his career was to be irredeemably intertwined with that of Pu Yi, for Doihara was to establish him as Emperor of Manchuquo.

Doihara's 'eyes and ears' at Peking in those autumn days of 1925 was *Shosa* (Major) Mino, who was charged with organizing the surveillance of Johnston. This was an easy enough task given the numbers of personnel available. All Japanese legations abroad were centres of espionage. As the 1920s developed increasing numbers of Japanese Imperial Army officers swarmed over the Kwangtung peninsula and Manchuria. In their wallets their identification papers described them as 'tourists on sightseeing trips', but cameras and military issue field-glasses and copious note-taking revealed their true purpose. Manchuria was to be the touchstone of Japanese expansion in the Far East. By 1919 they occupied two-thirds of it and Johnston's old stamping-grounds south-east of Peking. Already the 1931 Japanese invasion of Manchuria was anticipated by Japan's emergent warlords and Pu Yi was being eyed up for a future role in Japan's *Dai Toa Kyozonken* (Great East Asia Co-prosperity Sphere). Mino's task, as well as watching Johnston, was to see whether and how he might be recruited for Japan's cause. His closeness to Pu Yi might be exploitable.

Japanese intelligence reports concerning Pu Yi and Johnston also linked the tutor with other expatriates who worked in foreign and colonial service jobs and who might be manipulated in the Rising Sun's grand plan. They were particularly interested in those identified by undercover agents as being named on British diplomatic staff lists as 'Suspicious persons' and who might be susceptible to blackmail. One such was E.T. Backhouse.[6]

Sir Edmund Trelawney Backhouse (1873–1944) had been educated at Winchester and Merton College, Oxford. Although he did not take a degree or sustain his training as an orientalist, he had studied Russian and Japanese as an interest during his early years of wild-oat sowing and found himself in China in 1899 having fled from bankruptcy proceedings. His flair for languages helped him learn both written and spoken Chinese, and he kept himself busy in Peking with translation work for British officials (although he never became a member of the consular service). Backhouse worked as a researcher and translator for the Scottish-Australian *Times* correspondent Dr George Ernest Morrison (another of Johnston's acquaintances and correspondents), and probably through Morrison's patronage Backhouse was appointed a part-time teacher in the *I-hsueh kuan* (College of Languages) at the recently founded University of Peking in 1903. Backhouse dubbed himself 'Professor of Law and Literature'.

An ignominious blotch on Backhouse's none-too-pristine character occurred during the Boxer rebellion when he was accused of looting and was imprisoned by the Russians. His mistake was to steal artefacts from the area of the Forbidden City that the Russians themselves were systematically dismantling. On his release Backhouse moved into the British sector of the Imperial City into a portion of a house belonging to a court official called Ching-shan, Assistant Secretary of the Imperial Household, who had been murdered, aged seventy-eight, by his son a few days previously on 15 August 1900. The name Ching-shan was to be a controversial and recurring theme in Backhouse's life ever after.

By 1908 Backhouse was also helping John Otway Percy Bland, former secretary to the Municipal Council of Shanghai, with research and reports again for *The Times*. Together they were to collaborate on a book which came out the same year (1910) as Johnston's *Lion and Dragon in Northern China*. Entitled *China under the Empress Dowager*, the book was centred around the diary of His Excellency Ching-shan, which Backhouse apparently found in his new lodgings. The diary was later dismissed as a complete forgery. Even so, the book was published in Britain by William Heinemann and was a great success. Johnston was one of the Chinese scholars who accepted the diary's authenticity.

During 1912 Johnston had become 'chief supporter' of the Anglo-Chinese League. This group of learned enthusiasts was to be based 'at some mountain shrine' to study Chinese religion and culture.[7] Johnston heard from Walter Perceval Yetts, the medical officer at the British Legation in Peking, that Backhouse, now regarded as a prominent Chinese scholar, had just presented his library of 17,000 books (to which another 10,000 volumes were to be added) to the Bodleian Library in Oxford. Johnston would have liked the books for the League, which, in the event, was to die through lack of interested parties.

Described as 'one of the outrageous forgers, confidence tricksters and eccentrics of the century', Backhouse had lovers of both sexes; he boasted relationships with both Gladstone's Secretary for Foreign Affairs, the 5th Earl of Rosebery and the Empress Dowager, as well as various of her eunuchs.[8] Johnston knew Backhouse well, but denied repeatedly that he had 'any acquaintance' with him. The lies were to become obvious because Imperial Court group photographs showed them together. Japanese agents reported that Johnston and Backhouse – who was a keen collector of erotica – were often to be seen together in the brothels near the British Legation across from the Mongol Market.

Latterly an antipathy had grown up between Johnston and Backhouse for reasons unknown. Certainly Backhouse was scathing about Johnston's scholarship, while Johnston's true feelings about Backhouse, if recorded, were destroyed at his death.[9] In the meantime, Backhouse and Johnston were linked in the files of Japanese Military Intelligence.

* * *

Johnston notes in *Twilight in the Forbidden City* that at no time during his stay at the Japanese Legation (and later at Tientsin) was Pu Yi invited to go to Japan, even though his pupil 'would have rejoiced at the opportunity of exchanging his drab and colourless life'.[10] Moreover: 'On the contrary, it was intimated to him, through me, that his presence whether in Japan or in the Japanese-leased territory of

Kwangtung in Manchuria would "seriously embarrass" the Japanese government.'[11] Johnston's statement of the patently obvious discloses a naivety that is astonishing in view of the political awareness he displays elsewhere in the book. It was not 'serious embarrassment' that was the key, since the Japanese were clearly beginning to size up Pu Yi at close quarters for the role they had planned for him in the future of Manchuria. For them to invite him to Japan would have revealed too much of their hand to the more percipient diplomat. Already a steadily growing anti-Japanese feeling was abroad in China and it was not in Japan's interests openly to court Pu Yi beyond playing generous host.

Within the Japanese Legation the Japanese main 'fifth columnist' was one Lo Chen-yu. A scholar and dealer in antiques (many of them misappropriated from the imperial collection by the *Nei Wu Fu*), Lo had held an honorary post 'in the imperial secretariat' at the Imperial Palace.[12] His job now was to persuade Pu Yi to throw in his lot with the Japanese; being Chinese Lo could easily propagandize such a move as the will of the Chinese people. Lo was responsible for Pu Yi being moved to the Japanese Concession at Tientsin, where he would remain from February 1925 to November 1931.

At about this time Johnston received a letter from Stewart Lockhart asking whether he would like to be considered for the chair of Chinese at London University.[13] Stewart Lockhart was a member of the governing body of what is now the School of Oriental and African Studies, and was keen for Johnston to be involved in the furtherance of Chinese scholarship. Johnston declined. He did not want to leave his pupil during this transition stage, and it was likely that he would be called back to Weiheiwei. In the meantime he wrote to his old colleague concerning the events of the 'Emperor's Flight' and subsequent transfer to the Japanese Concession at Tientsin.[14]

Before leaving for Tientsin, Pu Yi held a court reception to mark his nineteenth birthday.[15] The reception room at the Japanese Legation was transformed into a 'state room', and the Japanese authorities provided yellow furniture and trappings to imitate imperial splendour. The pro-monarchy guests attended bedecked in court finery; Johnston joined them in his acquired regalia. It was a very emotional and somewhat pathetic event for the still young 'Lord of Ten Thousand Years'.

The melancholy stirred up by Pu Yi was heartbreaking as the procession of his old loyal Ch'ing dynasty courtiers, whose aged limbs could hardly perform the rituals, sank to the floor in the nine-fold *kowtows*. As the old men were hoisted to their feet Pu Yi could barely retain his tears. As the last courtier backed away Pu Yi addressed the company.

He gave a summary of his feelings as a guest of a friendly country that had given him succour when he escaped from his life as a 'prisoner'. He regretted his impounded (still at the Forbidden City) 'clothes, vessels, calligraphy and books left by my ancestors'. The Japanese diplomats stood impassively as he concluded: 'I will never agree to any proposal that I should seek foreign intervention on my behalf: I could never use foreign power to intervene in domestic Chinese politics.'[16] The assembled company remained silent when Pu Yi had finished, until a ripple of polite applause that started among the foreign guests was swept into huge acclaim, encouraged by the Japanese delegation.

A few days later Pu Yi and an attendant cycled out of the Japanese Legation to visit the Forbidden City. Minister Yoshizawa was furious. Not long after Pu Yi learned what his new 'freedom' meant: when he attempted to cycle out of the compound once more the Japanese guards barred his way and refused to open the gate. In the usual deferential terms he used whenever he addressed the ex-emperor, Minister Yoshizawa explained that these security measures were for his own good. His hosts, hissed Yoshizawa, feared for their honoured guest's life in the turmoil in the city.

Pu Yi realized that one prison had been exchanged for another; it would be the same for the rest of his life. This was the cue for Lo Chen-yu to put the idea into his head of a move to 'safer, less expensive' Tientsin. With Minister Yoshizawa and his staff bowing him out – with many regrets that he felt he had to go – Pu Yi and Johnston boarded a special train from Peking's Chienmen railway station on 23 February. The Japanese plan for Pu Yi was running smoothly. Curiously, in his book Johnston only retells the events of the move from Peking. Uncharacteristically he says nothing of any advice he gave to the emperor and expresses no opinion about the move's significance.

This was the first of a lengthy series of goodbyes for tutor and pupil. Sitting together in the private carriage as Japanese security men passed up and down the corridors, they reviewed the times they had spent together and the events of the past six years. Here he was 'on the run again', opined Pu Yi, just like Bonnie Prince Charlie, whom Johnston had talked about in their classroom discussions on Scottish history. Pu Yi had been fascinated by the story of Prince Charles Edward Stuart's flight from the battlefield of Culloden in 1746. Would he himself be the hero of such a romantic tale in years to come?

From 4 May 1919, in response to news from the Paris Peace Conference that the Allies intended to 'give' Shantung to Japan, Pu Yi and Johnston had experienced another layer of turmoil in Peking mirroring the widespread demonstrations organized by youth groups. This 'May Fourth Movement' inspired people such as Mao Tse-tung, a founder of the Chinese Communist Party in 1921, to agitate for a Marxist-Communist Revolution to redress the 'wrongs' perpetrated in and against China. Such events made Pu Yi's hopes of restoration even bleaker and Johnston's sadness even more poignant that there was little he could do to help his pupil in the long run.

On 7 April 1921 Dr Sun Yat-sen was elected President of China at Canton, but the country remained divided north–south in warlord rivalries. International extraterritoriality rights continued to weaken China and Johnston was a keen supporter of the allies 'giving back' much that they had appropriated from China's landmass. In January 1924 Dr Sun Yat-sen's *Kuomintang* (Nationalist Congress) had formed a government in Canton and allied itself with Communist groups.

General Feng Yu-hsiang had turned on his allies by 24 November 1924 and seized Peking, giving the Japanese an excuse to bar their compound gates for Pu Yi's 'own good'.

On their journey Johnston and Pu Yi discussed the tutor's immediate future. Pu Yi was not in a position to pay his tutor's salary, and it was time for Johnston to resume his career in the Colonial Service. He did not tell Pu Yi that Britain's interest in the ex-emperor had waned still further. The British Foreign Office considered that the coming man was General Chiang Kai-shek, who would in a few months succeed Dr Sun Yat-sen after his death at Peking on 12 March 1925. Johnston was not downhearted by his immediate prospects, as he hoped to play a part in the 'giving back' process that he had advocated for so long.[17]

Finally, Johnston and Pu Yi arrived at Tientsin, which in those days was China's most international city after Shanghai. A Treaty Port since 1861, the British, French and Germans had laid out concessions to the south of the Chinese city, and in 1895 the Japanese had set out their own concessions.

On arrival they were surrounded by a phalanx of Japanese secret policemen in plain clothes and when the Japanese guard of honour had presented arms and the Japanese *Soryoji* (Consul General) Shigeru Yoshida had uttered a formal welcome, they were hurried to the Japanese concession.

Lo Chen-yu had already arranged their accommodation at the *Chang Yuan* (Chang Garden), a three-acre walled estate on Asahi Road, in the heart of the Japanese concession, opposite the headquarters of the Japanese Secret Service at Kasuga House. From now until the end of the Second World War Pu Yi would be followed by plainclothes policemen.

As the Chang Garden house was not quite ready, an overnight stay was made at the Japanese-owned (and easily monitored) Yamato Hotel. Johnston knew that Pu Yi already had a 'safe house' in Tientsin, where he had hidden imperial artefacts and a cache of money when he was planning to flee to England. The emperor had wanted to stay there, but as it was in the British concession and the British government had refused him police protection, Johnston stayed with Pu Yi at the Yamato Hotel. Disputes about the apportioning of the Chang Garden's two-storey mansion's better rooms started almost immediately among Pu Yi's retinue.

Pu Yi confided to Johnston that he considered his Tientsin sojourn to be temporary until he could take up their 'joint dream' of England and ultimately Oxford. Johnston expressed hope that this project would come about, believing in his heart that it was impossible.

Johnston said his farewells to Pu Yi at Tientsin and embarked on the next phase of his career. In 1926 he became secretary of the British China Indemnity Delegation, under the chairmanship of Freeman Freeman-Thomas, 1st Marquess of Willingdon, and former Governor of Bombay, then Madras. The delegation was concerned with Britain's share of the monies to be paid because of the Boxer uprising. The negotiations necessitated Johnston's return to Britain, for only the second time in twenty-eight years. Before he did so he visited Pu Yi again at Tientsin and went the rounds of influential Chinese, including the warlord Wu Pei-fu, in an effort, largely unsuccessful, to drum up support for his pupil's cause.

Early in 1927 Johnston returned to China as British Commissioner at Weiheiwei. This appointment was the culmination of another of Johnston's 'dreams' for China. He was greatly in favour of the reversion of the territory,[18] and he had made no bones about it to all who would listen.[19] Before taking up this post on 31 March, Johnston was back in Tientsin with Pu Yi. Johnston recalled: 'I remained [at Weiheiwei] until the British government carried out its long-standing promise to restore the territory to China nearly four years later . . . during the time I kept in touch with the emperor and paid him several visits.'[20] On one occasion Pu Yi persuaded him to try out one of the new motorcycles he had purchased. A tentative Johnston wobbled precariously around the compound while Pu Yi dissolved into great mirth.[21]

Johnston told his friend Stewart Lockhart that he had in his employ at Weiheiwei one of Pu Yi's servants 'for the purpose of acting as an intermediary if I want to communicate with the emperor without using the Post Office'.[22] His visits and communications with Pu Yi were something of an on-going irritation to the diplomats at the British Legation in Peking, who feared that his 'meddling' would draw him – and ultimately the foreign service – into potentially embarrassing Chinese political intrigue. They went so far as to call him into the legation and warn him off.[23] Johnston listened politely with 'the indulgent smile he has used since he was a little laddie in Edinburgh when he has no intention of complying', and took no notice.[24] Alas, Johnston failed to advise his pupil to be wary of the Japanese, who were slowly brainwashing his immediate staff and advisers in the belief that the Dragon Emperor could never be reinstated on the Dragon Throne without the assistance of the Imperial Japanese Army.

In 1928 Johnston was awarded the CMG (Companion of the Order of St Michael and St George). During this year Pu Yi was becoming more personally in thrall to the Japanese. He decided that his brother Prince Pu Chieh, who had come with him into 'my exile', and his brother-in-law Jun Ch'i would better serve him if they spoke good Japanese. *Soryoji* Yoshida suggested Takeo Toyama as their tutor, and an unsuspecting Pu Yi was steadily drawn further into the maelstrom of politics, factions and secret societies that would bring Japan to war.

Toyama was a member of the Japanese *Kokuryukai* (Black Dragon Society) which was founded in 1901 with the purpose of pushing the Russians out of Manchuria.[25] In his *Journal*, Pu Yi reveals that earlier in 1925, through the encouragement of Lo Chen-yu, he had met Nobuo Tsukuda of the *Kokuryukai*, described by Lo as one of the 'many powerful people in Japan . . . planning to help me achieve my restoration'. The *Kokuryukai* organized agents to keep up gunfire outside the Chang Garden to intimidate Pu Yi into being more dependent on the Japanese security services.

The Japanese treated Pu Yi with the respect due to a reigning monarch. He was invited to functions, visited at New Year and on his birthday by the *Soryoji* and senior officers from the local Japanese garrison. His photograph was circulated to all Japanese senior officers of the Army and the Navy so that he could be easily recognized for proper salutes and greetings. He was even given due deference by the most feared of Japan's counter-intelligence services, the *Kempeitai*. Invitations came his way to attend military parades such as the Japanese Emperor's Birthday Parade while the commanding officer of the garrison regularly visited him to give briefings on Japanese activities in China. One such was *Chusa* (Lieutenant-Colonel), later *Chujo* (Lieutenant-General), Yasunori Yoshioka, who was later to become his military attaché in Manchuquo. The briefings were loaded with propaganda, criticizing the Chinese Army and highlighting the superiority of the Japanese way of government, and emphasizing how 'the hearts of the people of China could only be won' by Pu Yi mounting once more the Dragon Throne.

* * *

In the closing years of the 1920s Reginald Fleming Johnston encountered romance again in the form and personality of Eileen Power. Born 9 January 1889 at Dunham Massey, Bowden, near Altrincham in Cheshire, Eileen Edna le Poer Power was one of the three daughters of Philip Ernest Le Poer Power, a stockbroker jailed for fraud, and his wife Mabel Grindley Clegg. Educated at Bournemouth and Oxford High Schools, and Girton College, Cambridge, she graduated in 1910 and soon became one of Britain's leading academic historians, being particularly known as a medievalist and an early pursuer of 'women's history'. From 1913 to 1921 she was director of studies in history at Girton, then lecturer (1921) and reader (1924), taking a professorship of economic history at the London School of Economics from 1931.

During 1921 Eileen Power went on a two-month trip to China through a Khan Travelling Fellowship; it was the first time a woman had held such a benefice. She travelled from Singapore to Hong Kong, and thence to Canton. She visited the Western Hills, and while at the monastery of Chieh T'ai Ssu on a 'walking tour' with a Miss Harding, she became aware of 'Mr Johnston's place' (Cherry Glen).[26]

Commentators have speculated that 'an unsatisfactory father' had contributed to her preference for older men. In 1921 she was thirty-two and Johnston was forty-seven. They became fascinated with each other; she because of his knowledge of the ancient China she was bent on studying, and he for her beauty, her intellect and enthusiasm for the literary interests he shared. Power was particularly taken by the way Johnston grafted traditional Chinese thought on to his own mode of thinking. He showed her the 'spirit tablets'[27] he had set up in the temple he had constructed at Cherry Glen, dedicated to his favourite poet and muse Percy Bysshe Shelley, and introduced her to the ways of the *suan kua hsien-shang* (diviners) and his fascination with Chinese spiritualism.[28] He also loaned her a horse to facilitate her explorations of his valley and hills.[29]

Power left an account of her visit in her work *The Haunted Valley*. She notes how 'the scholar [Johnston] had escaped from the man-built walls of the city' to the 'protection and peace' of the hills. Here he constructed his dwelling on an elevation in a glen between two hamlets.

> Life slips away here in the haunted valley, haunted indeed by peace. Sometimes the scholar sits alone, reading old poems by T'ao Yuan-ming and Po Chu-I and Li Po, or pondering old philosophies.[30] Sometimes he bids other scholars to be his guests, old men so learned and so revered that they must be borne swaying along his paths.[31]

Eileen Power made a second trip to China in 1929, and once again came under the influence of Johnston. A mixture of amicability and attraction developed into love and a marriage was discussed. Johnston was to write to Stewart Lockhart: 'I have a . . . charming person . . . staying with me at present, namely Miss (!!!) Eileen Power . . . I met her when she visited Peking 7 years ago & again when I was in London 3 years ago . . . She is spending a fortnight with me – Miss Walkinshaw being the only chaperone.'[32] Eileen Power then continued her travels to Japan and Manchuria but was to take up her relationship with Johnston once he had returned to Britain.

During the summer of 1929 the novelist Stella Benson spent some time at Cherry Glen; as a friend of Power's she was aware of Johnston's feelings for Eileen and recorded her impressions of him. He was 'much simpler and more accessible to public opinion than I remembered', she said. 'Somehow, since he is so much cleverer than anyone else in China, a nest of legend seems to have formed itself around him, and it is surprising to find him at the core of that . . . a flesh and blood person.'[33] Johnston was to encourage that 'nest of legend' around him for the rest of his life.

* * *

Although dogged by Japanese security men, Pu Yi and his wife Elizabeth lived an almost sybaritic life in Tientsin after saying farewell to the respected *Chuan Shih-tun*. They became prominent socialites, attending a range of events from the Scottish St Andrew's Society Ball to visits to places under the disguise of 'Mr and Mrs Wang', sometimes accompanied by a British journalist in Tientsin, *The Times* correspondent Henry Woodhead, whose writings Johnston had used in his English language tutorials with Pu Yi.

Before leaving Pu Yi in Tientsin, Johnston had introduced him to the most senior of Britain's diplomats, who paid various courtesy visits to Pu Yi's quarters. The appearance of succeeding commanders of the British garrison at Tientsin encouraged Japanese military intelligence and the *Kempeitai* to take more interest in Pu Yi. A report also went back to

Tokyo that the British royal family were continuing their interest in Pu Yi. The attention was innocent enough. When Prince Henry, Duke of Gloucester (1900–74), visited Tientsin in 1929, on his way to Japan, leading a mission to confer the Order of the Garter on Emperor Hirohito, he met Pu Yi and accepted a photograph of him as a gift for King George V. The king reciprocated through the British consulate.

As Pu Yi lived the life of what might be called Tientsin café society, spending huge amounts on Western goods, clothes and knicknacks, subbed by the considerable fortune of valuables, real estate and cash collateral he still retained, China was lurching from one crisis to another. By 21 March 1927 the forces of the *Kuomintang* had taken Shanghai, and captured Nanking on 24 March; in the latter conflict Chiang Kai-shek's General Cheng Chien's forces set upon foreigners with great barbarity in an orgy of rape, pillage, murder and mutilation. British and American destroyers shelled Nanking in order to rescue their nationals. Chiang's dream of a unified China moved forward. The communist forces, however, diverged from Chiang's policies and a rift with the Nationalists opened up. The young Mao Tse-tung retreated with several hundred peasants into the Ching-Kang mountains to hone his ideas for guerrilla warfare that were to conquer China twenty-two years later.

Slowly the Japanese were infiltrating Pu Yi's former empire; by 19 April 1928 there were 25,000 Japanese troops in Shantung alone. Pu Yi was now to meet in person Manchuria's most famous warlord Chang Tso-lin, who had been involved in the past in restoration plots on the young emperor's behalf. Clandestinely, although monitored by the Japanese Secret Service, Pu Yi slipped out of the Japanese concession to talk to Chang Tso-lin in the hope that he could rekindle any hope there might be of restoration. Nothing much relevant was discussed, but Pu Yi felt that he had opened up a useful door to his future. The next day he was rebuked by the *Soryoji* for the exploit, stressing that the Japanese could not be responsible for the emperor's safety if he persisted in trying to give them the slip. But there was more to it than that; although Chang Tso-lin had been a valuable ally to the Japanese they now considered him to be unstable. While Chang was travelling by train to Mukden his carriage was blown up by a team trained by *Taisa* Daisaku Komoto. Chang was killed instantly and on 3 June 1928 the Japanese announced that the warlord had been assassinated by 'bandits'. By 6 October, with the support of the warlords Feng Yu-hsiang, Yen Hsi-shan, and Chang Hsueh-liang of Manchuria, Chiang Kai-shek had won control of a unified China, and was declared president.

On 10 July 1929 the Chinese army seized the Chinese Eastern Railway in Manchuria, provoking Russian intervention; a compromise was agreed for joint management of the railways, and Japanese troops withdrew from China. At Tientsin Pu Yi continued his costly lifestyle, but reflected, even in his most optimistic moments, that he was never likely to be restored.

During July 1929 Pu Yi and his entourage removed themselves into another quarter of the Japanese concession called the Quiet Garden. Once his work at Weiheiwei was completed Johnston went back to Tientsin to say a grand farewell to Pu Yi. In *Twilight in the Forbidden City* Johnston described their meeting:

> He came to my hotel very early in the morning of my departure – September 15th, 1930 – and remained with me till it was necessary for me to go on board my steamer. We drove together in his car to the wharf, and he sat in my cabin till the last possible moment. It took nearly half an hour for the steamer to turn round before going down stream. During that time he sat in his car on the wharf and remained there as long as the ship was in sight.

Johnston made no comment about his final conversation with Pu Yi on this occasion, nor the obviously desperate situation into which China was falling. Instead he dwells on the last gift that Pu Yi gave him: a fan on to which Pu Yi had copied an old Chinese poem of farewell. This was to be one of Johnston's proudest possessions and he regularly went back to read its poignant calligraphy:

The road leads ever onward,
And you, my friend, go this way, I go that.
Thousands of miles will part us –
You at one end of the wide world, I at the other.
Long and difficult is the journey –
Who knows when we shall meet again?

The Tartar horses breathe the northern winds,
The birds of Yueh build their nests in southern trees.
Our farewells are said, we are far apart;
Already I grow weak with pining.
The sun is hidden by the drifting clouds,
The traveller journeys on, turning his head no more.
Thinking of you, I seem to have grown old.
The months have swiftly passed, a whole year has gone.
It is all over. There is no more to be said,
I must make myself strong for the strenuous days to come . . .

Out of the city's eastern gate I go on foot,
To gaze longingly at the road that leads to far Kiangnan
On that day of storm and snow,
Here it was that we parted, and my friend went away.
I want to follow him across the river,
But the river is deep and has no bridge.
Oh that we were a pair of herons,
That we could fly home together.[34]

Immediately after the reversion of Weiheiwei on 1 October 1930, Johnston returned to Britain aboard HMS *Sandwich*. That year he became Sir Reginald through the award of Knight Commander of the Order of St Michael and St George.

CHAPTER 7

TWILIGHT IN BRITAIN: THE RELUCTANT DON

Johnston was to return unexpectedly to China around a year after his leave-taking with Pu Yi. This was partly because of his involvement in the Boxer indemnity business, and partly because the biennial Pacific Conference was to be held in China that year. A few days before his ship docked in Japan, Japanese troops moved out of the railway zone they controlled in Manchuria and attacked Chinese troops, whom they accused of blowing up a piece of track on the Japanese-owned South Manchuria Railway. Later known as the Mukden Incident of 18 September 1931, the action was a clear violation of the Kellogg-Briand Pact of 27 August 1928, which was signed by the USA and fourteen other nations, including Japan, to outlaw war as an instrument of national policy. It clearly indicated Japan's acquisitive intentions towards mainland East Asia.

Days later Johnston's ship crossed the East China Sea to Shanghai and he was in Tientsin on 7 October where he immediately joined the emperor. At this time various senior Imperial Japanese Army officers were being introduced to Pu Yi's circle as a part of the plan to lure him to Manchuria; one such was *Taisa* Kenji Doihara who had ordered the surveillance of Johnston some years previously. Doihara was a key member of the group of Japanese officials who were now pressurizing Pu Yi to 'answer the call of his people to lead them out of the darkness caused by the warring warlords'. Doihara slowly but deliberately fed Pu Yi the line that he must first establish himself as ruler of Manchuria and then he could emerge as emperor of a new united China. The latter would be under Japanese suzerainty, but naturally Pu Yi was not told this part of the plan. All of these encounters with the Japanese Pu Yi recounted to Johnston, whose advice (if any) to his pupil was never recorded (or if it was, it was destroyed after Johnston's death).

After pursuing his official business in Peking, Johnston was back with the emperor on 15 October, and then went on to his duties at the Pacific Conference. In *Twilight in the Forbidden City* Johnston remembered: 'The Chinese press at that time was full of rumours that the emperor was about to ascend a Manchurian throne. My own supposed influence over him was mentioned in several of the papers, and I was approached by some Chinese who wished me to use that influence in dissuading him from leaving Tientsin.'[1] At no time is there any indication that Johnston ever made efforts to persuade Pu Yi not to comply with Japanese suggestions.

By 10 November Johnston was in Nanking when he received an urgent summons from acting Minister of Foreign Affairs, T.V. Soong. He showed Johnston a telegram from the northern army command area stating that Pu Yi was 'in danger and in need of Johnston's help'. It was clear that the Commander-in-Chief of the Japanese Kwaitung Army, *Taisho* Shigeru Honjo, was preparing for military action in Manchuria. This could precipitate an attempt to kidnap Pu Yi by the Japanese, or perhaps even assassination by the idiosyncratic Chinese resistance groups. Through Soong, and clearly with Chiang Kai-shek's authority, it was hoped that Johnston could persuade Pu Yi not to cooperate with the Japanese. Johnston replied to Soong: 'the emperor [knows] of my movements and [can] communicate with me direct at any time. If he were in danger and needed my help, he has only to say the word and I would go to him. But the word must come from himself.'[2]

Three days later Johnston learned that Pu Yi had left Tientsin for Manchuria. To counter persistent (mostly Chinese) assertions that the Japanese had kidnapped Pu Yi, Johnston wrote those fateful words in

Twilight in the Forbidden City that would cause Pu Yi so much difficulty when his probity was at stake when testifying at the war crimes trial: '[The emperor] *went to Manchuria of his own free will.*'[3]

It is clear that Johnston approved of Pu Yi's defection. At the time he was putting the final touches to his book *Twilight in the Forbidden City*. He told Pu Yi that he would delay publication until his pupil was on the way to being installed as Emperor of Manchuria so that he could round off the book with a glorious chapter on Pu Yi's restoration under the title 'The Dragon Goes Home'.[4]

Throughout it is likely that Pu Yi believed that Johnston was acting with official backing of the British Foreign Office and of the British royal family he so admired. This false assumption was supported when the British garrison commander Brigadier F.H. Burnett-Nugent sent Pu Yi his 'personal congratulations' on the 'opportunities' now open to him. Johnston's naive attitude, and his blinkered stance towards the Japanese, had pushed his pupil further into danger and secured his life in another form of 'prison'.

* * *

When Johnston returned to Britain he bought himself some new clothes, installed himself in a house at Eversfield Road in Richmond, Surrey, and gave long consideration as to what he wanted to do with the rest of his life. He was still bitter about what he regarded as a poor deal he had received over advancement in Hong Kong. Writing to his friend the colonial specialist Lionel George Curtis, who brought about the foundation of the Royal Institute of International Affairs in 1920–21, he complained that Sir Miles Wedderburn Lampson, Minister at Peking from 1927 to 1933, had 'blasted' his opportunity to become Governor of Hong Kong on the retirement of his old Magdalen fellow student Sir Cecil Clementi in 1930.[5]

To a large extent his lack of preferment was due to his being 'difficult'; he was regarded as a colonial 'loose cannon' and his penchant for playing the *poseur* did not help. On his return to Britain Johnston brought with him the traits of great eccentricity, a desire to be a recluse, and what could be an irritating affectation. In the London clubs where sinologists and 'old China hands' of the commercial cadres gathered, Johnston's reputation was discussed and analysed.[6] His rumoured position as 'a fully ordained Buddhist priest' was mulled over, while others averred he was 'of ill-balanced mind'. In all he was to become a figure around whom many legends both accurate and inaccurate would be woven.

As his correspondence was to show over the years, from his first colonial employment as Weiheiwei, an academic lifestyle was not anathema to Johnston, although in those early days it would have been most congenial in a Buddhist retreat on some holy mountain mentioned in his travelogues. For years he had been monitoring academic billets from Hong Kong to Columbia which he had applied for in 1917.[7]

The chair of Chinese studies at London University's School of Oriental Studies being vacant, Johnston was urged to apply for it by such people as W.E. Soothill, the ex-missionary Professor of Chinese at Oxford, who was one of the SOS electors. Affecting a forced modesty – 'I am very doubtful about my qualifications for such a post. I am not really a Chinese scholar – I merely know a few words of Chinese and can recognize a few Chinese characters when I see them' – Johnston eventually applied for the post.[8]

On 3 March 1931, with a majority vote of the SOS electors – among whom were his old friend Stewart Lockhart and Walter Perceval Yetts, who had helped him compose his *curriculum vitae* – Johnston was selected for the post, defeating his main rival (and ultimate successor) the Chinese scholar Evangeline Dora Edwards.

Johnston was not happy at being 'elected' to a post by a voting system; to him it was a humiliation. His six years in the position were to prove an anti-climax to his career. In the first place Johnston was not a trained professional academic and he was not up to date in his

Chinese scholarship; moreover Evangeline Edwards and her supporters, including Johnston's predecessor J. Percy Bruce, were constantly breathing down his neck.

He was to take up his new post during the 1931/32 session. Although he was a scholar, Johnston was not taken with teaching; he was bored giving tuition in colloquial Mandarin; having to repeat lecture materials irritated him, as did the putting together of lecture notes; he loathed the department's administration work, and he tended to lapse mid-lecture into reminiscences of his heyday at the Imperial Court and his self-assessed role therein. Even though he continued with his writing and publishing, Johnston succumbed to laziness as far as university work was concerned, and all this spilled over into heated rows with his colleagues.

Why had he taken the job? He would much rather have taught at Oxford – but an Oxford lectureship only paid £80 per annum, while at London he was offered £1,000. His personal funds had been depleted by financial difficulties in China's economy, and his pension prospects were reduced because of his 'time out' with Pu Yi. Further there was also his love for Eileen Power to consider; she was firmly based in London and his finances would have to stretch to keeping a wife. His Scottish sense of independence would not have had it otherwise.

* * *

'I don't profess to understand women and don't know how to deal with them,' Johnston had written to Stewart Lockhart in August 1931.[9] Because of these feelings Johnston seemed to find it difficult to make the final commitment to marriage. Yet soon after Johnston returned to England, Eileen Power was telling her friends that they were engaged and she wrote to her friend Margery Lois Garrett that 'My toreador's ring is *greatly* admired here.'[10] An air of disillusionment began to develop for Eileen when she viewed the furnishings Johnston had gathered for their proposed marital home at Eversfield Road; it was a mixture of contemporary furniture and the priceless curtains and antiques that Johnston had been given by Pu Yi.

The proposed wedding date of January 1931 went by as the 56-year-old Johnston procrastinated. So undecided was he that by the summer of 1931 the marriage was off. Johnston explained to Stella Benson: 'I finally decided not to [marry] because I had a strong feeling that for Eileen's sake it was very much better that we should not be married.'[11] Those who knew Johnston well were not surprised by such events. Although the engagement to Eileen Power was broken off, their friendship continued and there was some talk of rekindling the relationship towards marriage. However, Eileen Power had had enough of this on-off situation and by February 1932 all future matrimonial plans were scuppered.

As time went by Johnston, who had been deeply in love with Eileen Power at Weiheiwei, gave her a few of the 'imperial treasures' he had amassed in China, and he remembered her in his will. Not long before Johnston's death, Eileen Power married her former research assistant Moissey Postan in December 1937. She died of a heart attack on 8 August 1940.[12]

Johnston continued his unsatisfactory career at SOS and from late 1932 to 1934 he played host to Pu Yi's second sister Princess Jun-ho, who in 1932 married T.K. Cheng, the son of the cultured loyalist civil servant Cheng Hsiao-hsu. Their first child Ying Tsai was born in London on 15 February 1933 at a house owned by financier Sir Robert Hotung.[13]

Around the time that his engagement to Eileen Power came to an end, Johnston became restless and talked about settling down for his retirement in Devon or Cornwall.[14] What changed his mind is not clear, but his thoughts eventually turned to his homeland and the west coast of Scotland where he had gone as a schoolboy to visit family friends. On 8 October 1934 he bought from Colonel Edward Donald Malcolm the three islands Eilean Righ, Eilean Nan Gabhar and Island Macaskin in

Loch Craignish, all being parts of the estate of Poltalloch, Kilmartine, Argyllshire.[15] Here, within a complex of two houses, set opposite to each other in a rectangle, Johnston hoisted the Manchu flag and laid out his home surrounded by his Chinese artefacts. The main island of Eilean Righ Johnston transformed into a little China of temples and 'views'. His domain, sustained by an idiosyncratic system of gas and electric generation, was run by six to eight local retainers. Once this bolt-hole was secure, Johnston began to plan a trip to see his old pupil.

* * *

After Johnston had left Pu Yi in 1931, the emperor began to mull over the reasons why he should go to Manchuria and take up the Japanese offer. Doubts began to set in. He was receiving no support from his now neurasthenic and opium-smoking wife Elizabeth, whose mood swings, tantrums and depression had caused them to drift apart; in her loathing for the Japanese she did not savour being in their power by debt or protection. Pu Yi's advisers, too, averred that a transfer to Mukden would be unwise until the Japanese had completed the conquest of Manchuria. So Pu Yi stayed put.

On the direct orders of *Taisa* Kenji Doihara the mental pressure on Pu Yi was stepped up. The task of increasing the secret service penetration of Pu Yi's household staff was given to secret policeman *Shosa* Takayoshi Tanaka. Tanaka chose his own lover to be chief coordinator of the new phase of subversion. Eastern Jewel was a daughter of Prince Su of the Manchu imperial house, and as her father had been driven out of temporary rule of Mongolia he had thrown in his lot with the Japanese. Eastern Jewel had spent some time in Tokyo and had led rather a shady life, but as a relative of the Manchus she had been a houseguest of Pu Yi's in the late 1920s.

Donning men's clothes at will, Eastern Jewel – known to the Japanese as Hoshiko Kawashima – played her part well in the intimidation of Pu Yi. She made sure that he received forged letters threatening his assassination prepared by Doihara, who also blackmailed Pu Yi's old friends into telephoning him with warnings of his planned murder. While Pu Yi still hesitated, Eastern Jewel saw to it that two repellent (but harmless) snakes were placed in his bed. She also 'discovered' two bombs placed in a basket of fruit sent to Pu Yi by an old acquaintance. Eastern Jewel sent for the *Kempeitai* to take charge of the bombs with much brave theatricality. Later 'investigations' by Japanese criminologists showed that the bombs 'had been manufactured in the arsenal of Chang Hsueh-liang', the former warlord of Manchuria whose partisans, the Japanese said, were gunning for Pu Yi.

On the same night that the bombs were 'discovered', 8 November, Doihara planned a series of riots in the Chinese quarter to back up Eastern Jewel's latest pressure on Pu Yi's fears. To heighten the tension the Japanese garrison commander ordered the Quiet Garden to be cordoned off. This time Eastern Jewel was successful with her persuasive threats and the emperor agreed to flee. In a bizarre escape plan – which mirrored his farcical flight from the Forbidden City with Johnston – Pu Yi was bundled into the boot of his convertible. The Japanese sentries and armoured car cordon of the Quiet Garden made the driver of the escape car so nervous that he reversed the car into a telephone pole. Pu Yi, already in the boot, received a bang on the head which left him dazed throughout the trip.

At last the car swung into the courtyard of a Japanese-owned restaurant on the fringe of the Japanese concession. Released from the boot, Pu Yi was dressed in a Japanese Army greatcoat and forage cap and was bundled into a staff car and taken to the docks in the British concession and put aboard a motor launch in the River Pai. Pu Yi was stowed away in the vessel's bilges next to a drum of high octane gas fuel – which was fused to incinerate him if the plan went wrong. Finally they set off towards the Gulf of Chihli past the Chinese defences. They were challenged by a Chinese patrol boat but after a feint the helmsman raced away to their rendezvous with the Japanese merchant vessel *Awaji Maru*.

Next day they arrived at the Yingkow docks which belonged to the South Manchuria Railway Company and were now in the hands of the Japanese. Pu Yi was welcomed ashore by the secret police thug *Tai-i* Masahiko Amakasu and taken to a spa outside Port Arthur and thence to the Yamato Hotel at Mukden. By December Eastern Jewel had persuaded Elizabeth to join Pu Yi and they were to live together, although emotionally distant from one another, until the Japanese were ready for the next stage.

In his own mind Pu Yi had convinced himself that the Japanese intended to restore the Manchu Dynasty within a new great Ch'ing Empire. On 18 February 1932 Manchuria was declared an 'independent country', with Japanese control behind the scenes; the Japanese dubbed the country *Manchuquo* (Land of the Manchus). On 15 September Japan proclaimed Manchuria a protectorate.

By 25 February the Japanese had installed Pu Yi as *Ch'ang ch'un* (Chief Executive) of Manchuquo, but internationally all was not well. On 2 October a League of Nations commission of inquiry, led by the British statesman Victor Bulwer-Lytton, who had been Governor of Bengal from 1922 to 1927, issued a report denouncing the 'rape of Manchuquo'. The commission recommended an independent government for Manchuquo under Chinese sovereignty with international administrators and police. Japan's diplomatic response was hysterical fury, and by 1933 Japan had withdrawn from the League of Nations. In March 1934 Pu Yi was promoted to Emperor of Manchuquo under the new name Kang Te. Changchun (renamed Hsingking, or Shinkyo to the Japanese) was set up as his new capital city. A disillusioned but compliant Pu Yi accepted enthronement, but it was not to be in the fine and colourful robes of his first coronation: after a perfunctory ceremony in Chinese dress, he wore the uniform of the Commander-in-Chief of the Manchuquo Imperial Army for the Japanese induction. Internationally Pu Yi's humiliation was complete, and he appeared as a puppet emperor during his April 1935 state visit to Japan.

Pu Yi had kept in touch with his former tutor and at his prompting Johnston applied in May 1935 for a leave of absence from SOS to visit Manchuquo. In his usual fashion he let it be known at the Foreign Office that he would be delighted to carry out research or enquiries on their behalf during his visit. The Foreign Office chiefs rejected Johnston's overtures. Those within its corridors of power who rather liked the 'eccentric old buffer' were afraid for his safety should he be given official status; those who saw him as an 'arch-meddler' feared that he would cause diplomatic embarrassment. At worst, the Foreign Office China Desk averred, the Japanese secret services, who would monitor him all the time he was in their area, could easily trump up espionage charges against him, but with no official status His Majesty's Government would not be compromised.

Although Johnston made it clear to all he met in Manchuquo that he was on a private visit to his old pupil as well as carrying out some personal research – he went on to study the Manchu archives at Mukden – he was *de facto* a guest of the Japanese puppet government. He was hosted throughout by the *Jikan Gaimu-Daijin* (Japanese Vice-Minister for Foreign Affairs) and was given an official luncheon. He was taken on tours of Japanese prestige developments and projects, his every comment of praise for the Japanese being noted down; yes, Manchuquo was a fine launching-pad for his pupil's restoration to the Dragon Throne. After his visit to Pu Yi, Johnston went on to Japan, Hong Kong, Indo-China, Malaya and the Dutch Indies – areas that within a few years would fall to the brutal onslaught of Japanese militarism. His appetite for travel satisfied, Johnston made a leisurely voyage home.

His attitude towards the Japanese became ever more eccentric. As Robert Bickers pointed out, he even tried to persuade the *Nippon Taishikan* (Japanese Embassy) in London to utilize his *Twilight in the Forbidden City* 'for pro-Japanese "propaganda purposes"', even listing those entries which best promoted Japanese interests.[16] A Japanese edition of Johnston's book was published in Japan in 1935. To many who knew him Johnston seemed finally to have gone too far when he boasted that his pupil had

> returned to the land of his fathers – a land which his family had never ceased to regard as 'home' – and has resumed the imperial style and status of Manchurian emperor. He has done what that veteran Chinese statesman T'ang Shao-yi declared in 1925 that he was entitled to do – having been rejected and thrown out by the Chinese people he has resumed possession of the 'rightful heritage' which had been the dowry brought by his Manchurian forefathers to the China-Manchurian union.[17]

Thus Johnston fabricated a complete fantasy background for what was a very tenuous – and very dangerous – position for Pu Yi. Because of all this Johnston infuriated Chinese students in London and earned the contempt of fellow-Chinese scholars, particularly at SOS. All of which, of course, gave him a certain pleasure.

On his return to London, Johnston formally indicated to SOS that he did not wish his appointment to the chair of Chinese to be extended after the 1936/37 session. On 29 June 1937 he officially retired and took himself back permanently to his Scottish roots.

CHAPTER 8

Dragon at Bay: Dead Witness for the Prosecution

Some time in the 1930s Reginald Fleming Johnston met Mrs Elizabeth Sparshott, the daughter of George and Elizabeth Tebbitt of Grand Avenue Mansions, Hove, Sussex.[1] According to those who knew her well Elizabeth Sparshott 'was a woman of rare beauty, sharp perception, and great intelligence'. She had been married once and had one daughter, Jessica. Local tradition in Beckenham has it that during the early 1930s she had become 'besotted' with another man and had left her husband and daughter to live with him in Spain. On his death in around 1935 she returned to Britain and her association with Johnston began.[2]

Johnston and Sparshott now set up home together at Eilean Righ, which was renovated in oriental style and dubbed by Johnston 'The Temple to the Unknown God'. In correspondence with his lawyer friend R.A. Robertson, Johnston described Sparshott as his wife 'in all but name', and explained how they ran the estate together, sharing expenses.[3] From time to time they set off on jaunts to favourite places like Crieff and Pitlochry, and sailed and picnicked off the west coast of Scotland. Johnston added membership of the Royal Highland Yacht Club to his associations.

Annie Mackenzie, whose father had worked on the old Poltalloch estate, remembered as a teenager delivering goods by boat with her father from Ardfern to Eilean Righ.

> I remember the little yellow boats that used to be drawn up on the foreshore of the island where Sir Reginald had set up little statues of Buddha, I suppose, among the rocks. It was the Emperor of China's sacred colour, he said.
>
> One day he said to my father: 'Come on, Mackenzie, and look at my new garden.' In the yard beside his house he had planted a poppy garden that was now in full flower. The garden reminded him of the hills and wild flowers around his house in China. We always knew when Sir Reginald was at home for he hoisted a yellow flag [of the Emperor of Manchuquo] by his house.[4]

In 1936 Johnston's health began to deteriorate and he had an operation for the extraction of a calculus from his ureter. He became more and more housebound at Eilean Righ, pottering among his books and the artefacts given to him by Pu Yi. He was admitted to the Royal Scottish Nursing Home at 19 Drumsheugh Gardens in Edinburgh and during February 1938 was operated on for the removal of a kidney stone.

Johnston died on 6 March 1938 of kidney failure, and was cremated at Warriston Crematorium, Edinburgh, on 8 March. His will had declared: 'No religious service of any kind is to be carried out at or in connection with my funeral.' According to his last wishes, Elizabeth Sparshott scattered his ashes on the waters of Loch Craignish.[5]

Johnston's death and association with Emperor Pu Yi were ultimately to have international consequences. First there was the will. In it he left everything to Elizabeth Sparshott, except for a few cash legacies to such people as his lifelong friend Professor David Heatley, Eileen Power, his niece Rosemary Fleming and his cousin Major Douglas Johnston. Specifically, he left his 'Sable Cloak and Chinese embroideries given to me by the ex-Emperor of China now Emperor of Manchuria' to Elizabeth Sparshott. It was his wish that his island home be given to the National Trust for Scotland when Elizabeth Sparshott had no further use for it. In the event, she sold the Eilean

Righ properties with their important salmon fishing rights to Major Archibald Campbell.[6] Island Macaskin went to Dr Frederick Cameron Sillar, and Eilean Nan Gabhar to James M.B. Wright.[7]

The contents of the will infuriated Johnston's sister Noney, who disputed the validity of the legacies. The solicitors J. & R.A. Robertson raised an Action of Declarator in the Sheriff Court at Dunoon and on 19 June 1938 the holograph will was declared legal.[8] Johnston's movable cash estate in Britain was accounted at under £2,000. The value of his artefacts at Eilean Righ were logged at just over £4,000, but the sales of the islands brought Mrs Sparshott several thousand more. And there was a 'Chinese element', too, in the estate which was accounted later.[9] Elizabeth Sparshott gave Noney some artefacts while the School of Oriental Studies received books, scrolls and pictures. Over the years Johnston had sent money to China to support festivals in the temples around Cherry Glen and for the families of his former house servants. Now Elizabeth Sparshott gave money gifts to the inhabitants of the villages adjacent to Cherry Glen, Ying T'ao Kou, Tao Yuan and Nan Chuang.[10]

Slowly, obituaries of Johnston began to appear, mostly in learned journals, but none revealed many details of his personal life. The *Daily Mail* dispatched a reporter to Argyllshire to track down the story of the man who had been tutor to the last Emperor of China, who was in the news as the puppet Emperor of Manchuquo. Although the reporter met Elizabeth Sparshott at Oban she refused to give any details of her relationship with Johnston and a bland paragraph appeared in the paper on 7 July 1938. All that Elizabeth Sparshott was ever to say publicly was: 'We were both lovers of nature, he especially. Indeed, I called him a child of nature, yet he was a genius in language and literature.'[11]

As far as the world was concerned that was an end to the matter until interest in Johnston was engendered by the Italian film director Bernardo Bertolucci's movie of 1987 entitled 'The Last Emperor'. It starred John Lone as Pu Yi and Peter O'Toole as Johnston. By then

Elizabeth Sparshott had been dead for almost a decade and Reginald Fleming Johnston's story had never been fully told. Yet the friendship between the reclusive Scotsman and the star-crossed boy emperor was to take an explosive turn a few years after Johnston's death.

* * *

Following Johnston's last farewell to Pu Yi in 1935, the emperor lethargically ruled over his troublesome Manchurian empire, disturbed by guerrilla and bandit activity. On 19 July 1936, after Chiang Kai-shek had won control of Kwangtung, there was a call by the regional Chinese warlords (and the Communists) to declare war on Japan. Chiang was not ready for such a move, but in early October Japan made commercial and military demands which threatened China's autonomy. The Nanking Government refused to agree to the demands although the nation was meant to feel intimidated by the presence of increased numbers of Japanese troops at Shanghai.

By 28 January 1937 the Shensi (Communist) Government and the Nanking (Nationalist) Government agreed to act together under Chiang Kai-shek to oppose Japan. On 28 July Japanese troops captured Peking; on 8 November Shanghai fell to the Japanese, followed by Nanking on 13 December. Although repeatedly attacked by guerrilla forces the Japanese declared China a protectorate on 25 September 1938 and the whole of the Chinese theatre spun towards the all-out war that followed the attack by Japanese planes on the US Pacific Fleet in Pearl Harbor in Hawaii on the morning of Sunday 7 December 1941.

The puppet emperor and his entourage usually heard about events in the war zones long after they happened. Manchuquo functioned under severe Japanese censorship and Pu Yi's sham court dwelt in a kind of information limbo. All they heard was a brief outline of Japan's 'war of liberation' and that the 'Japanese are good people with pleasant manners' and how the people of Manchuquo 'are very happy'.

Pu Yi reigned as puppet Emperor of Manchuquo for eleven years. In that time he went to Japan twice more, in 1940 and 1943. After 1938 he rarely ventured out of his palace in the old Salt Tax building at Changchun except to visit hospitals, factories and housing programmes, carefully propagandized by the Japanese. When the Second World War was declared in the Pacific Region, Pu Yi was given desultory briefings by his Japanese adviser *Chujo* Yasunori Yoshioka. Years later the ghost writer of his autobiography described Pu Yi's life as 'a kind of living death' as he slipped into mindless lethargy. He pretended to have forgotten most of the English Johnston had taught him and became subject to vicious mood swings which resulted in daily beatings for his staff.

Yet the tennis and bicycling Johnston had introduced to Pu Yi became some of his chief occupations as day succeeded endless day. His wife Elizabeth lived in an opium-fuelled world of her own inside the palace. In April 1937 Pu Yi had taken the sixteen-year-old Manchu girl Tan Yu-ling (Jade Years) as his *shu-fei*; she died in 1942 whereafter he married Li Yu-chin (Jade Lute).

Some time before his second visit to Japan, Pu Yi heard that his old tutor had died. He was shocked and tearful at the news. He brooded over the time that they had spent together, initially as pupil and teacher, and then as very close friends. He found it impossible to believe that he would never see Johnston again. How less dangerous and complicated his life would have been if they could have fulfilled their 'dream' of going to England together.[12]

Despite his existence in a world of Japanese propaganda nonsense, Pu Yi knew that the war was not going well for his masters. Although he knew it was dangerous, he began to tune in to broadcasts in Chinese beamed from American relay stations. From these he learned of the Japanese retreat in the Pacific and Burma. When *Taisho* Tomoyuki Yamashita, Commander-in-Chief of the Imperial Japanese 1st Army, paid a courtesy visit to report his recall to Tokyo, Pu Yi realized that the defeat of Japan was not far off.

The desperation of the situation was made more intense when for propaganda purposes Pu Yi was wheeled out to 'dedicate' a group of soldiers who would be 'human bullets'. These were the *nikudan* who would sacrifice themselves in last ditch attacks on any enemy soldiers who invaded Manchuquo. On 6 August 1945 the atom bomb was dropped on Hiroshima; on 9 August another fell on Nagasaki. On 8 August the Soviet Union had abrogated their recognition of the territorial integrity of the 'Empire of Manchuquo' and invaded. As Pu Yi was being briefed on the Soviet situation by *Taisho* Otozo Yamada, the new Commander-in-Chief of Manchurian troops, the air-raid sirens sounded over Changchun, scattering Pu Yi's hysterical attendants over the complex.

On 10 August it was decided that Pu Yi should be evacuated 'to safety' at Tunghua along with his entourage. Soviet bombing caused the train in which they were travelling to be re-routed to the mining town of Talitzou. There Pu Yi heard of Japan's capitulation. Between 18 and 22 August the Soviet Army took over the province and Soviet troops moved into Port Arthur and Dairen following the surrender of all Japanese forces in Manchuria by *Taisho* Yamada on 21 August 1945 at Changchun. Elsewhere civil war broke out in China between Chiang Kai-shek's Nationalists and Mao Tse-tung's Communists.

Two days before the Soviet victories in Manchuria, Pu Yi took part in another surreal ceremony of the sort that seemed to pepper his whole life. In the dining room of the two-roomed mining camp hostel in which he was staying at Talitzou, he formally renounced the throne of Manchuquo and proclaimed that his government, led by the Japanese-toady, Prime Minister Chang Ching-hua, was dissolved. Manchuria was returned to Chinese territory.

Pu Yi was now to go to Tunghua where he would board a plane with eight members of his family and *Chujo* Yasunori Yoshioka, his former aide. The plan was for him to fly on to Korea and thence to Japan, out of the clutches of the Soviets of whom Pu Yi was terrified. In his loathing for Bolshevism, Johnston had emphasized the horror of the slaughter of Tsar Nicholas II and his family at Ekaterinburg on the eastern slope of the Ural mountains on 16 July 1918. Thus to Pu Yi the Soviets were 'Emperor-Murderers' and he feared that he would be next.

While they were waiting at Mukden for the transfer flight to Korea, Soviet air force aircraft landed and occupied the airport. Once the landing strips and buildings were secured, the senior Soviet officer turned his attention to Pu Yi. Next morning he and his group were taken out to a Soviet plane bound for Khabarovsk on the Amur river, the second largest city of the Soviet Far East. When they stopped to refuel, Pu Yi accosted the most senior officer he could find. It had occurred to him that he must try to disassociate himself from his former Japanese puppet-masters. He boldly averred that he and his family would not travel with 'Japanese war criminals'. *Chujo* Yoshioka, his erstwhile aide, was accordingly removed from their party.

The Soviets began almost immediately to dismantle the economic and industrial state that the Japanese had built. They selected all the costly electric generator and locomotive power infrastructure that would be of use to the Soviet state and shipped it back to Russia. Everything else was destroyed. Meanwhile Pu Yi lived, half-prisoner, half-guest in a Russian spa-hotel near Khabarovsk, along with a clutch of Manchuquo generals, senior civil servants and ex-ministers. The Soviet authorities were uncertain what to do with him, and Soviet military intelligence interrogation of him was perfunctory. Stalin, however, ordered the retention of Pu Yi as a part of a future plan he had to seize Manchuria for the Soviet Union, while China was in civil war turmoil. Stalin believed that he could set up a puppet regime in Manchuria like the one he had established in Mongolia.

The rest of Pu Yi's companions were of little interest to Stalin. With Pu Yi was his brother Pu Chieh, but his wife Elizabeth, who had not travelled with them, died in prison at T'umen on the Korean border in June 1946 of malnutrition and the consequences of drug abuse. Jade Lute was released.

During March 1946, and guarded by a detail of Stalin's secret police, Pu Yi began the journey that was to take him to Tokyo to appear before the war crimes tribunal then being set up. The Russians were anxious that Pu Yi should be tried as a war criminal; this would help to put pressure on the Allies to force Emperor Hirohito of Japan to face similar charges. Stalin insisted that Pu Yi should be returned to Soviet custody after the trial, a proviso eagerly accepted by General Douglas MacArthur for the Americans. They feared that Pu Yi's lingering presence in Japan, as witness for or against the prosecution, would hinder their own plans for the rehabilitation of Hirohito.

Pu Yi was not to enjoy the good luck that attended his brother emperor. Acting on the orders of Democratic Party President Harry S. Truman, General MacArthur was to use Hirohito to unite a new Japanese state as a bulwark against Communism in the east. Pu Yi was doubly unlucky, for even Hirohito's relatives who had acted so bestially in Manchuria were to be exonerated by MacArthur. While Pu Yi had spent time idling as a puppet-ruler, Hirohito's father-in-law Prince *Chujo* Kuni spearheaded the Manchuquo germ warfare centre (the notorious human experimental depot, Unit 731); and while Pu Yi rode his bicycle and played tennis, Hirohito's uncle Prince *Chujo* Yasuhiko Asaka ordered the slaughter of 300,000 military prisoners in Nanking, for which *Taisho* Iwane Matsui took the blame.

On 3 May 1946 the first public session of the International Military Tribunal for the Far East, generally known as the Japanese War Crimes Trials, was called to order at the old *Rikugun Shikan Gakko*, Ichigaya, Tokyo, in a building that had been the headquarters of the Imperial Japanese Army during the Second World War. Here the story of Japan's genocide began to unfold: six million civilians had been killed by the Japanese on the Chinese mainland by the end of the war.

For eleven days in August 1946 Pu Yi sat as a prosecution witness in the dark-panelled former auditorium of the *Rikugun Shikan Gakko*, now transformed into a modern courtroom. His role was to testify to the 'brutalization' of Manchuquo by the Japanese; to the disgust and dismay of many he was not on trial himself. The proceedings were under the presidency of Australian High Court Justice Sir William F. Webb, who was an expert in Japanese atrocities; privately he believed that Emperor Hirohito was the worst of Japan's war criminals.

Pu Yi gave a remarkable performance on the witness stand. It was a brilliant display of braggadocio. The gawky, short-sighted, slow-thinking, rather cardboard cut-out figure that Johnston had tutored and written about was replaced by a man skilled in slyness, deception and artifice. His verbal tennis with Justice Webb, the US prosecutor Joseph Berry Keenan and the American and Japanese defence councils was masterly. He clearly saw himself as a defendant rather than a prosecution witness and acted out this role accordingly. He averred that *Taisho* Kenji Doihara's negotiator *Taisho* Seishiro Itagaki had threatened him with death if he did not accept the throne of Manchuquo. He blamed the West for being soft on the Japanese; even his tutor had admired them. He went on to explain that all he had done since 1931 had been under duress. And all he said was phrased in flowery Chinese, which was difficult for the official interpreters to translate because of the varying shades of meaning of the words he used. At length Justice Webb declared his impatience with Pu Yi's testimony: 'All day long we have listened to excuses by this man as to why he collaborated with the Japanese. I think I have had enough.'[13]

The US defence counsel Major Ben Bruce Blakeney (counsel for *Taisho* Yoshijiro Umezu, former commander of the Kwangtung Army) made his attitude to Pu Yi quite plain: 'I intend to impeach him . . . [he] desired, planned for, and eagerly seized the opportunity to obtain restoration to a throne.' Thus he geared up for a new line of enquiry. He now produced the link between Reginald Fleming Johnston and Pu Yi, his assistants having procured Johnston's volume *Twilight in the Forbidden City*. Johnston's words did not stand Pu Yi in good stead. For Blakeney, one passage in the book stood out. It occurred in the 'Epilogue' on page 450: '[Pu Yi] left Tientsin and went to Manchuria of his own free will.'

Blakeney asked Pu Yi if he had felt badly done by by the Chinese Republic and had removed himself from the Forbidden City in 1924. Their dialogue is given below:

Pu Yi	My feeling then was that I would rather move out of the Forbidden City because the circumstances there were not wholesome at all. This situation was fully recorded in Mr Johnston's *Twilight in the Forbidden City* from which you can understand my feeling and my situation.
Blakeney	Then we may assume, may we, that Sir Reginald Johnston's book correctly expresses your viewpoint?
Pu Yi	Yes, rather correctly.

Pu Yi now began to see a large chasm opening up into which he could easily fall.

Blakeney	I should like you to tell us just what his [Johnston's] position was.
Pu Yi	He was my English tutor.
Blakeney	Did he serve you for a good many years?
Pu Yi	Yes.
Blakeney	In addition to being your tutor, was he also your friend and adviser?

Pu Yi began to see that Johnston's book and friendship was to be of no help to him.

Pu Yi	He was merely a tutor of mine.
Blakeney	Was he quite familiar with all the details of your life and your opinions during the period he was with you?
Pu Yi	For ordinary times, he knew a bit about me. But after I went to Manchuria he didn't know anything about me.

This is blatantly untrue. Even allowing for exaggeration on Johnston's part the old tutor kept up with happenings in Manchuria even when in London.

Blakeney	I believe you stated that in his book he correctly stated the circumstances of your life?
Pu Yi	In that book there were many sections . . . I never had the occasion to read the whole book . . . as far as the section describing my life in Tientsin, I didn't know what he was writing about.
Blakeney	When was the last time you saw Sir Reginald Johnston?
Pu Yi	The last time I saw him was in Manchuria.
Blakeney	When was that?
Pu Yi	I cannot recall the date or the year.
Blakeney	When was the last time you saw him before leaving Tientsin?
Pu Yi	To tell you frankly, I cannot recall these dates. Since I cannot recall, I cannot tell you.
Blakeney	Did you see him within about a month before the time you left Tientsin for Port Arthur?
Pu Yi	I cannot recall.
Blakeney	Did you write a preface to his book?
Pu Yi	I cannot recall that.

Blakeney now produced a copy of Johnston's book and read the Preface from it. He emphasized the words: 'No one has a more intimate knowledge than he of the disasters and hardships of that critical period.' A transcript was handed to Pu Yi.

Pu Yi	This was written by Cheng Hsiao-hsu [the scholar-poet who became Prime Minister of Manchuria under Pu Yi]. It was not written by me.[14]

Blakeney	Do you mean that the calligraphy is not by you or the words are not yours?
Pu Yi	I have never seen this.

At this point the US Prosecutor Joseph Keenan contested the use of material by Johnston as the old tutor was dead. Although the objection was sustained by Sir William Webb, Blakeney managed to quote a further passage from Johnston's book as, he said, it cast grave doubts on Pu Yi's credibility as a witness for the prosecution. Blakeney cited Johnston's account of the conversation he had with Pu Yi just before the emperor left Tientsin for Manchuria and asked if it were true.[15]

Pu Yi	At that time Johnston was, as a matter of fact, in Tientsin. But there was no such conversation. Johnston wrote this book with a commercial end in view. He [wanted] to sell this book for money.

Pu Yi thus suggested that his old friend and tutor was a liar and that *Twilight in the Forbidden City* was a complete fabrication. Blakeney then turned to articles written by Henry Woodhead based on interviews with Pu Yi, and the Japanese defence counsel introduced poems that Pu Yi had written. All these showed that Pu Yi had been a willing tool in the hands of the Japanese, and his testimony was thus proved to be unsound. Again luck was on Pu Yi's side. Sir William Webb terminated the cross-examination of Pu Yi, ruling that its continuance would be 'utterly useless'. Pu Yi left the courtroom and was handed back to his Soviet guards to be returned to Khabarovsk. He had escaped the gallows which awaited several of the twenty-eight Japanese war crimes defendants who had had close dealings with Pu Yi in Manchuquo.[16]

EPILOGUE

To the Heavens Dragon Borne

On his return to Khabarovsk and Soviet detention, Pu Yi learned that Chiang Kai-shek had sent a mission to Moscow to petition for his extradition to China. This was unsettling news, for Pu Yi believed that the Nationalist leader would certainly mount a show trial and have him executed as a traitor to China. Soviet policy concerning Pu Yi would save his life once more. To them he was a valuable spoil of victory, and Stalin had no intention of handing him over to the vulnerable, anti-Communist Nationalists. Soviet intelligence was watching Mao Tse-tung closely and reported that Mao would win the struggle to secure China for extreme socialism. For the moment the Soviets slid the bolts behind Pu Yi.

From his comfortable spa hotel, Pu Yi was moved to Detention Centre no. 45, based in former school buildings near Khabarovsk. Here he mixed with Manchuquo and Japanese senior officers and civil servant detainees, but was allowed extensive privileges and escaped fatigues. Pu Yi's father-in-law Jung Yuan acted as general steward, directing his former emperor's staff of attendants and keeping an eye on Pu Yi's substantial imperial possessions. As he whiled away his time Pu Yi wrote letters to Moscow asking for political asylum in the USSR. His letters remained unanswered.

News percolated through to Pu Yi that Shanghai had fallen to the Communists, who proclaimed the North China People's Republic on 1 September 1948. By 15 January 1949 the Communists had occupied

Tientsin; on 21 January they entered Peiping, whereupon Chiang Kai-shek resigned. On 1 October the Communist People's Republic of China was proclaimed, with Mao Tse-tung as its Chairman and Chou En-lai (1898–1976) as Premier and Foreign Minister. The USSR recognized the new regime immediately.

Pu Yi was confident that the Soviets would not execute him but he was very anxious about Mao's Communists. He had learned about socialist systems of government from Johnston (who had despised them) and the Manchuquo Prime Minister, his former Chinese tutor, Cheng Hsiao-hsu, and about the Chinese Communists in particular from the latter and from his erstwhile Japanese colleagues. What he had learned from them did not fill him with confidence. After all, the Communists considered him to be 'the epitome of all that had been evil in the old Chinese society', as their press regularly confirmed. Yet in truth, what the new rulers of China set out to do was not to murder Pu Yi, as their Soviet neighbours had the Romanovs, but rather to rehabilitate him as a Communist. This policy was supported and commended by the new Premier Chou En-lai.[1]

Pu Yi was returned to China by the Soviets on 31 July 1950. All the time he felt that the execution squad was getting nearer, and that every day might be his last. He interpreted the kindly treatment of his guards during his transfer as keeping him docile and happy as death approached. At length Pu Yi arrived at Fushun prison in Harbin, which had been built by the Japanese in 1936 to house political prisoners: it was now the Chinese Communists' 'Thought Control Centre'. Pu Yi became prisoner no. 981, but was regularly allowed to see members of his family including his father-in-law Jung Yuan, his brother Pu Chieh and three nephews. Fears of impending execution gradually began to fade from his mind.

Along with Kuomintang generals, Japanese and Manchuquo war criminals, Pu Yi endured the 24 hour Marxist-Leninist-Maoist brainwashing programme. He underwent exhaustive interrogation on Japanese and Manchuquo war crimes, and wrote 'confessions' of his years in Manchuquo wherein every act by the Japanese had been done in his name; he was faced with the horrific story of the Japanese occupation, events about which he had known little or nothing. Pu Yi suffered bullying and harassment from fellow prisoners, but as he was 're-moulded' into a citizen of the People's Republic he emerged as a 'model worker' and, although retaining his penchant for clumsiness, he became humble in mien, zealous in undertaking his tasks and self-deprecating.

During September 1959, the tenth anniversary of the foundation of the People's Republic of China, Mao Tse-tung ordered an amnesty for certain categories of prisoners. An official of the Supreme People's Court read out the 'Notice of a Special Pardon' to assembled prisoners at Fushun:

> The war criminal Pu Yi, aged 54, of Manchu nationality, and from Peking, has now served ten years' detention. As a result of remoulding through labour and ideological education he has shown that he has genuinely reformed. In accordance with clause one of the Special Pardon Order he is therefore to be released.[2]

On 9 September 1959 Pu Yi arrived at Peking's railway station to be met by his half-brother Pu Ren. The last phase of his life had begun. He became more absent-minded, feckless and clumsy than usual. A significant event that took place not long after his release was his inclusion in a party of ex-prisoners taken to the Forbidden City as part of a Communist Party 'Familiarization Tour'. It was the first time that he had been back to his old home since he had left it with Johnston in 1924.

For the curious party visiting the Forbidden City that day, Pu Yi fell into the role of guide. He was astounded at the transformation that had taken place. The seedy, derelict place he remembered had been refurbished as a vast museum. He was later to write his impressions of his visit in the Communist Party magazine *Luyou* ('Travel'). He was allowed to seek out people in Peking whom he had known, such as his now bedridden octogenarian former adviser Chang Yen-ying. But now, as he affirmed to all, he was a loyal citizen of the Communist state.

A highlight of this later phase of his life was Pu Yi's encounter with Premier Chou En-lai which flowered into a lasting friendship. During an early meeting after his release Chou En-lai had had a special word with him. 'You weren't responsible for becoming Emperor at the age of three, or for the 1917 attempted restoration *coup*. But you were fully to blame for what happened later. You knew perfectly well what you were doing when you took refuge in the Legation Quarter, when you travelled under Japanese protection to Tientsin and when you agreed to become Manchuquo *Ch'ang ch'un*.'[3] Pu Yi humbly agreed: the brainwashing had succeeded.

During early 1960 Pu Yi took part-time employment as an assistant at the Botanical Gardens, a department of the Chinese Academy of Sciences, Botanical Institute. Around this time too he began to work with the ghostwriter Li Wenda on his autobiography *From Emperor to Citizen*, a task historians believe came from a suggestion from Chou En-lai. In many ways Pu Yi's work was a token gesture: he did cleaning chores in the hothouses and pricked out seedlings, but most afternoons he spent with Li Wenda at the Fragrant Hills Hotel working on his book. Their lunch bills were picked up by Chou En-lai's office.

Pu Yi worked on his book for four years, and in 1962 he became an archivist employed by the Chinese People's Political and Consultative Office. In this year, too, he won full citizenship of China along with their phoney voting rights; he also remarried, this time to Li Shusien whom many considered a government plant.[4] The year in which his book was published, 1964, Pu Yi underwent exploratory surgery to remove a kidney, and cancer was diagnosed. His next few years were to be filled with operations and by 1967 he was in a private ward at the Capital Hospital, Peking. Cancer of the bladder was now diagnosed, and he was well looked after on the orders of Chou En-lai, although this was the time of the beginning of the turmoils of the Cultural Revolution. Pu Yi died on 17 October 1967, as Red Guards rampaged through the hospital. His body was cremated on hospital premises. Because of the unstable events in China, Pu Yi's relatives were not able to collect his ashes until 1979. Thereafter his remains were buried at the Eight Treasure Mountain some 20 miles from Peking.

* * *

Thus passed the survivor of the pair who featured in this remarkable story. Theirs was one of the most curious relationships in the social history of late imperial China. Johnston had witnessed at first hand the metamorphosis of China from the indifferent, picturesque, conceited, abstruse, disconcerted and secluded nineteenth-century Manchu Empire, through a republic browbeaten by warlords, to a military dictatorship much of its territory having being seized by the Japanese. He had watched his pupil lead a kind of charmed if desultory life, from emperor to ex-emperor to emperor again, in a series of locations and events that formed virtual prison after virtual prison. All of this he had lovingly, if self-importantly, recorded in the book *Twilight in the Forbidden City*, which remains his finest epitaph.

Pu Yi had once looked upon Johnston as a respected father-figure, but portrayed him as a villain in his autobiographical *From Emperor to Citizen*. Pu Yi pictures Johnston as a vain man, always keen to pose prominently in official photographs, and a seeker of imperial honours to flaunt on every occasion possible. He accused Johnston of luring him away from all that was best in Chinese culture, from music to literature, to embrace instead Western imperialism, British brass bands, books and all things foreign. In emphasizing the greatness of the British Empire, wherein Johnston deemed himself 'the most learned member', Pu Yi said Johnston had explained how the Chinese people longed for Pu Yi's reinstatement as emperor. (At this point in the autobiography the propagandist ghostwriter noted that what the people of China really wanted was a Communist republic, and that Johnston, fearing this and stimulated by Western interests, pressed for Pu Yi's defection to the Japanese.) Overall, Pu Yi's brainwashing was complete with this cheap and cruel ridiculing of his trusted old friend; yet even without the brainwashing Pu Yi had turned against Johnston in his war crimes trials testimony. To several of his biographers this revealed him to be a basic poltroon.[5]

What was the truth? Did Johnston push his pupil uncaringly into the arms of the Japanese? To those who are not aware of Johnston's deep love of, perhaps his obsession with, China, this would appear the case. Yet it must be realized that Johnston was horrified when all he regarded as good, strong and rich in old China was destroyed by the modernizing influences of Republic, Nationalist and nascent Communist movements. Naively, some have said, Johnston saw the Japanese as a means to reinstate Pu Yi's credibility in a policy that would revitalize the old ways of China. That China had already died, but its demise Johnston never accepted.

When he had first entered the Forbidden City to take up his duties as tutor, Johnston's intention had been to mould Pu Yi into a Confucian gentleman, invigorated by the late Victorian love of a healthy, active outdoor life. This he tried earnestly to do, but fooled himself perhaps into believing that he had helped form a gentlemanly monarch who could rule with dignity and refinement. The 'gentlemanization' of Pu Yi was to be as shallow as Johnston's success as a diplomat, thwarted at the end for an ambassadorial chair or governorship, or indeed as a high-flying academic. Instead he inhabited a world of shadows, and dreams of what might have been. Yet Johnston remains a man of legend, the bulk of whose life was lived in the eye of the storm that raged through Asia and which formed a new nation that Johnston would neither have recognized nor been happy to live in.

GLOSSARY

For English-language material there are three systems of romanization in widespread use in defining Chinese terms, namely 'Post Office', 'Wade-Giles' and *Hanyu pin-yin*. The Wade-Giles system was formulated by Sir Thomas Francis Wade (1818–95), assistant to Lord Elgin, who undertook Chinese missions in 1857 and 1860, and who was British Minister at Peking 1873–74, along with Dr Herbert Alan Giles (1845–1935), a consular official in China 1867–93, and later Professor of Chinese at Cambridge 1897–1932. The Pin-yin style was devised in the 1950s and came into use in the People's Republic of China foreign language publications on 1 January 1979. These produce a divergence of spellings in English language books on China, for example:

Post Office	*Wade-Giles*	*Pin-yin*
Peking	Pei-ching	Beijing

Wherever possible, spellings that would be recognized in Reginald Fleming Johnston's day have been used, *but without stress marks*. Japanese words are marked [J].

Aisin-Gioro	'Golden Race'; clan name of the Manchu emperors
Boxers	See *I Ho Ch'uan*
Ch'ang ch'un	Chief Executive (See also next item)
Chih Cheng	Chief Executive
Ch'ing	The last dynasty of Imperial China. Founded by the Manchus, it ruled from 1644 to 1911
Ching Hua Min Kuo	Republic of China

Glossary

Chuan Shih-tun — Reginald Fleming Johnston's Chinese name
Chujo [J] — Army Rank: Lieutenant-General
Chun-tzu — Gentleman
Chusa [J] — Army Rank: Lieutenant-Colonel
Da Ch'ing Da Huang Ti — 'Great Emperor of the Great Ch'ing Dynasty': Pu Yi's ceremonial title. He was also known as 'Lord of Ten Thousand Years'; 'He Who is Above'; 'The Enthroned One'; 'The Lord of Myriad Years'; 'The One Who Faces South'; 'The Celestial Emperor'; 'The Emperor of Cathay'; and 'The Emperor of the Middle Flowery Kingdom'. He shared with Hirohito, the Emperor of Japan, the age-old imperial title of 'Son of Heaven'
Da Nei — 'Great Within' of the Forbidden City, the prerogative of the imperial court
Da Yunhe — Great Canal
Dai Nippon Teikoku Rikugun [J] — Imperial Japanese Army
Dai Toa Kyozonken [J] — Great East Asia Co-Prosperity Sphere
Danshaku [J] — Baron
Fan Ch'ing T'ung Meng — Anti-Manchu League
Feng-huang — Bridal symbols for happiness and prosperity
Feng-shui — 'Wind and Water'; the cosmic pseudo-science of geomantic harmony, wherein location, human life and artefacts are so arranged to bring good spiritual forces to bear on daily life
Feng-yu — 'Bridal seat'; the Phoenix Chair
Forbidden City — For a glossary of key features see page 57
Fou — 'Floating'; a term used to describe Emperor Pu Yi's day-dreaming in class
Gensui [J] — Army Rank: Field Marshal
Hanlin Yuan — Library of Chinese Scholarship, Peking
Hong — A licensed trader, or his commercial firm. They were under the control of their guild, the *Cohong*
Hsieh En — Formal thanks as expressed by the emperor
Hu Bu — Board of Finance

Hu Chun	Palace guards
Huan kuan	'Castrated man'; a eunuch
Huang shang	'His Imperial Majesty'; form of address
I Ho Ch'uan	'Society of the Righteous and Harmonious Fists'; a secret society dubbed the Boxer Movement by Westerners
I-hsueh kuan	College of Languages
Jen	Spirit of humanity; goodness. A Confucian ethic
Jikan Gaimu-Daijin [J]	Vice-Minister for Foreign Affairs
Joho-kikan [J]	Military Intelligence Department
Kempeitai [J]	Military Police
Kokuryukai [J]	Black Dragon Society
Kowtow	The 'three kneelings and nine prostrations' required of those approaching the emperor in audience. It began as a requirement for non-Chinese when tribute was being brought to the emperor. Asian peoples accepted the obeisance, but Western diplomats and traders refused to comply
Kung nu	Maid servants
Kuomintang	Chinese National Party, founded by Dr Sun Yat-sen in 1911
Lao Fo-yen	'Venerable Buddha'; name given to the Empress Dowager Tzu Hsi
Lao Tsu Tsung	'Venerable Ancestor'; epithet given to the Empress Dowager Tzu Hsi
Lin Shao-Yang	A pseudonym used by Reginald Fleming Johnston in his anti-missionary writings
Lung	Imperial five-clawed dragon
Lung-t'ing	'Dragon pavilions'; carrying chairs
Mandarin	Derived from the Portuguese *mandare* [to order], this is a general Western term for a Chinese official of provincial or lower rank. The term was used to describe the (northern) standard Chinese spoken by such officials, the *Kuan-hua* (official speech)

Manchuquo [J]	'Land of the Manchus'. The Japanese term for their puppet state
Manchus	A Tungusic tribesfolk who rose to power in the sixteenth century. They slowly extended their influence, from a humble beginning on the periphery of China's state and culture, to conquer Mongolia, Korea and areas of North China. In 1636 they declared themselves the Ch'ing Dynasty
Miao-hao	Temple name for the emperor
Nei T'ing	Inner Court [circle]
Nei Wu Fu	Imperial Household Department
Nien-hao	Reign name for the emperor
Nikudan [J]	Suicide soldiers – the 'human bullets'
Nippon Taishikan [J]	Japanese Embassy
Nu kuan	Ladies-in-waiting
Pan shih ta ch'en	'Commissioner in Charge'; Johnston's position at the Summer Palace
Pan-tu	'Companion readers'; a term used to describe the emperor's fellow students
Pao	'Treasure'; the severed part of a eunuch's anatomy
Rikugun Shikan Gakko [J]	Army Academy
Shosa [J]	Army Rank: Major
Shu-fei	'Secondary consort'; concubine
Sori-Daijin [J]	Prime Minister
Soryoji [J]	Consul general
Suan kua hsien-shang	Diviners of the supernatural
Ta Cheng Li	Marriage ceremony rites
Tael	Chinese currency. In Johnston's day 1 *tael* was equal to three shillings sterling
T'ai fei	Dowager consorts
T'ai Fu	Grand Tutor
Tai-i [J]	Army Rank: Captain
T'ai-hou	Empress Dowager
Taiping	'Supreme Peace'; combatants of the Taiping Rebellion 1850–64

Taisa [J]	Army Rank: Colonel
Taisho [J]	Army Rank: General
Ti Shih	Imperial Tutor
T'ien-tzu	'Son of Heaven'
Tsung Kuan Nei Wu Fu Ta-ch'en	Comptroller of the Imperial Household Department
Tsungli Yamen	Foreign Ministry
Tze-chin-ch'eng	Purple Forbidden Palace, Peking
Wan-sui-Yeh	'Lord of Ten Thousand Years'; one of the more frequently used of the emperor's titles
Yang kuai tzu	'Foreign Devils'; expression used for foreigners by Chinese extremists
Yu-ch'ien t'ai chien	Eunuchs of the Presence
Yu Hua Yuan	Imperial Garden
Yuan Ming Yuan	Summer Palace

FAMILY TREES

Genealogical Table of Sir Reginald Fleming Johnston's Immediate Family

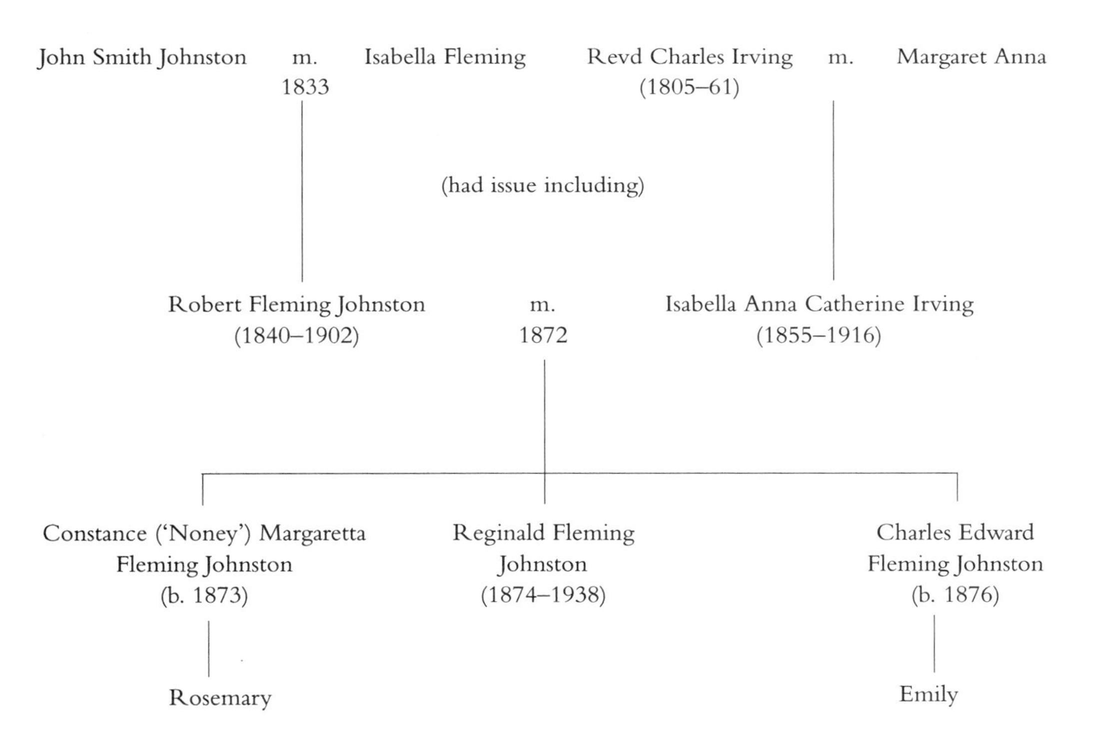

Dynasty of the Manchu Emperors – Dynastic Title 'Ta Ch'ing'

(Simplified to show main characters mentioned in the text)

T'ai Tsu [Nurhachi] 1550–1626, founder of the dynasty; ruled Manchuria as T'ien Ming

Succeeded by seven emperors then

Yi Wei
[Prince Yin Chih]

issue

Hsien-feng
r. 1851–61

m.
(as secondary consort)
Tzu Hsi

T'ung Chih
r. 1861–75

m.
Alute and
concubines
no descendants

Yi Hsin
[Prince Kung]

issue

Yi Huan
[Prince Ch'un]
1840–91

m.
Tzu Hsi's sister and
then a concubine

Kuang-hsu
r. 1875–1908

no descendants

Prince Ch'un (d. 1951)

m.
daughter of Jung Lu

Pu Yi
[Reign title: Hsuan-T'ung]
Emperor 1908–12
b. 1906 d. 1967
Head of State Manchuquo 1932–34
m. Wan Jung [Elizabeth] 1922
m. Wen Hsiu ['Number Two
Wife'], div. 1931 d. 1950
m. Tan Yu-ling [Jade Years] d. 1942
m. Li Yu-chin [Jade Lute] div. 1958
m. Li Shusien (1924–97)

Pu Chieh
[b. 1907]

Issue
inc: Princess Jun Ho
m. 1932 T.K. Cheng

Ying Ts'ai
b. London 1933

NOTES

INTRODUCTION

1. Alexander, Helen, *My Memories.*
2. A good background summary of the main events of the history of the years 1840–1927 in China can be gleaned by the general reader in Heren, Louis, *et al.*, *China's Three Thousand Years*, Part IV, Sections 1 to 5. For a more scholarly study see D. Twitchett and J.K. Fairbank (General editors), *The Cambridge History of China*, vol. II, Part 2.
3. Waley, Arthur, *The Opium War Through Chinese Eyes.*
4. Cheng, J.C., *Chinese Sources for the Taiping Rebellion, 1850–1864.*
5. Ashton-Gwatkin, F.T., *The British Foreign Service.*
6. Platt, D.C.M., *Cinderella Service.*
7. Coates, P.D., *The China Consuls.*
8. Wright, A. (ed.), *Twentieth-Century Impressions of Hong Kong, Shanghai and other Treaty Ports in China.*
9. 'Lorcha': a small vessel with European-style hull and Chinese-style sails.
10. Conroy, Hilary, *The Japanese Seizure of Korea.*
11. Michie, Alexander, *The Englishman in China during the Victorian Era*, vol. 1.

CHAPTER 1

1. Grant, James, *Old and New Edinburgh*, Cassell & Co., 1882.
2. Cant, Malcolm, *Villages of Edinburgh*, John Donald, 1987.
3. Now known as 24 Canaan Lane, Edinburgh.
4. Smith, Charles J., *Historic South Edinburgh*, vol. II.
5. *Writer to the Signet*: one of a society of solicitors at Edinburgh. They were originally clerks by whom signet (Crown) writs were prepared. In his daughter's Registration of Birth (1873), Robert Fleming Johnston is listed as 'Landed Proprietor', while his second son Charles Edward's entry (1876) gives 'Writer to the Signet'. The census of 1881 shows that the Johnstons retained three servants: Catherine Hart (housemaid); Marianne Sutherland (cook); and Rachael Grubb (nurse). Correspondingly in the 1891 census there are four servants: William Mitchell (gardener); Agnes Dixon (cook); Louise Shregers (Swiss-born ladies' maid); and Jane Fairweather (house and tablemaid).

6. General Register Office, Edinburgh. *Extract of Entries 1861–1965.*
7. Leslie, J.B., *Derry Clergy and Parishes* Donaghmore, 1937. Entry for installation, 12 October 1828, for Charles Irving (1805–61).
8. *Forfarshire*: The first meeting of Angus County Council was on 3 May 1928; before that the area was known as Forfarshire.
9. Robert Augustus Robertson was a correspondent of Reginald Fleming Johnston as family solicitor for many years. The firm of J. & R.A. Robertson (still extant at 15 Great Stuart Street, Edinburgh) was founded in the 1830s, and it is thought that Robert Fleming Johnston had a desk within their offices in his later and financially stretched years.
10. J. & R.A. Robertson, Edinburgh. *Correspondence Files*, 1912–18. Noney complained to Robert Augustus Robertson that her brother Reggie even signed his few letters to her with his initials as he would to a stranger. During 1907/8 Charles Edward Johnston served as Director of the Emma Willard Conservatory of Music, Plum Memorial Building, Troy Female Seminary; he is identified in the *Troy City Directory* (1907) as 'teacher'. To his family Reginald Fleming Johnston was 'Reggie', and to his Colonial Office colleagues 'R.J.'. His mistress (as she was dubbed by the Johnston family) Elizabeth Sparshott called him 'Reg' and his erstwhile fiancée Eileen Power called him 'Ref'. At the Chinese court he was Chuan Shih-tun.
11. Matriculation Form, 16 November 1894. *University of Oxford Archives*, UR1/1/23.
12. *Slater's Directory of Southport*, Schools section, 1887. The school was defunct by 1891.
13. The buildings of Falcon Hall were demolished in 1909.
14. Smith, Charles J., *Historic South Edinburgh*. Also *Edinburgh and Leith Post Office Directories*, vols 1886–92.
15. J. & R.A. Robertson, Edinburgh. *Correspondence Files*. Letter from Johnston to R.A. Robertson, 9 January 1903.
16. Heatley became Mackay Lecturer in History, University of Edinburgh, from 1900 until he retired in 1935; he died in 1944. He appeared as a beneficiary of £50 in Johnston's will.
17. Graduate finding aids, University of Edinburgh, and *Scholarships in Arts*, 1893–94.
18. University of Oxford, Matriculation Records, Michaelmas Term, 16 October 1894.
19. See note 15.
20. Letter to Sir James Lockhart from

Magdalen College, 5 December 1913, *Magdalen College Library*, MS 1084/1.

21. Markham, Sarah, 'Tutor to an Emperor', *Magdalen College Record*, 1988.
22. Reginald Fleming Johnston was Lewis Fry Visiting Lecturer 1933–34, where he lectured on 'Confucianism and Modern China'. *Office of the Registrar*, University of Bristol. The lecture was published as a pamphlet in 1934.
23. *Magdalen College Record*, 1911. Johnston was confirmed MA (Oxon) *in absentia*, 20 June 1901.
24. At that time all Civil Service examinations were dubbed 'trying for the Indian Civil Service'.
25. *The Times*, 8 March 1938: p. 18, Col B.
26. Bell, H.C.F., *Life of Palmerston*.
27. Benson, A.C. and Esher, Viscount, *The Letters of Queen Victoria*. Letters 1841.
28. A good overall history of the Crown Colony is assessed from Endacott, G.B., *A History of Hong Kong*.
29. Pope-Hennessy, James, *Half-Crown Colony*.
30. Ibid: this colonial life of Sir John Pope-Hennessy (1834–91), Governor of Hong Kong, offers a good picture of Victorian crown colony life.
31. *Moore Papers*: Estate of Mrs C.M. Moore.

CHAPTER 2

1. Obituary: *University of Edinburgh Journal*, 1938.
2. *Dictionary of National Biography*, 1931–40.
3. *Boxers*: so-named by foreigners because the *I Ho Ch'uan* performed athletic exercises similar to those of western boxers, but which were designed to stir up supernatural powers to make them invulnerable in battle. Contemporary Chinese called them *quanfei*, or 'boxing bandits', while in the Imperial Court they were referred to as *Yihetuan*, 'militia united in righteousness'. For an overall discussion of the Boxer movement see Martin, Christopher, *The Boxer Rebellion* and Cohen, Paul A., *History in Three Keys*.
4. For Johnston's comments on the Boxer emergency see his *Twilight in the Forbidden City*, Chapter III.
5. Ibid: Introduction.
6. *Foreign Office Documents*, China Desk, 1901, which Johnston quoted in the Introduction to *Twilight in the Forbidden City* from transcripts.
7. Wood, Frances, *No Dogs and Not Many Chinese*, Chapter 8.
8. Johnston's interest in folklore began about this time and he became a member of the London-based Folklore Society in June 1911, a membership he retained until his death.

9. J. & R.A. Robertson, Edinburgh. *Correspondence Files*, 1912–18. The firm carried on a running conflict with Mrs Johnston, and subsequently her daughter, in the apportionment of Johnston's allowance. Mrs Johnston also retained her servant Margaret McLeod, whom she obviously could not afford. Johnston even contacted the family doctor Burns Murdoch about his mother's state of mind; Dr Murdoch confirmed her compulsive spending as a 'disease'.
10. Shiona Airlie has produced the definitive biography to date on Sir James Stewart Lockhart: *Thistle and Bamboo*.
11. Couling, Samuel, *Encyclopaedia Sinica*: entries on Weiheiwei.
12. Johnston left a readable record of the history, village life, and legends of Weiheiwei in his *Lion and Dragon in Northern China*.
13. Barnes, A.A.S., *On Active Service with the Chinese Regiment*.
14. Wright, Arnold (ed.), *Twentieth-Century Impressions of Hong Kong, Shanghai and other Treaty Ports in China*.
15. Johnston, R.F., *Account of a Journey in Shantung from Weiheiwei to the Tomb of Confucius*.
16. Kong Demao and Ke Lan, *The House of Confucius*.
17. The Estate of M.I. Johnston: family papers and jottings. Johnston also had a cousin, Major Douglas Johnston of Bishopcote, Dornoch, who was a legatee in Johnston's will. The major was in receipt of letters and photographs from Johnston in China, but none survived the Major's death without heirs.
18. Ibid.
19. *Puisne Judge*: as in a petty court. See: *Lion and Dragon in Northern China*.
20. *The Estate of M.I. Johnston*. Johnston became a member of the Royal Highland Yacht Club, Oban.
21. J. & R.A. Robertson, Edinburgh. *Correspondence Files*, 1907.
22. Ibid: 1 May 1912.
23. *Daily Press*, 31 August 1911.
24. Letter to Sir Herbert Warren, from Peking, 21 May 1923: *Magdalen College Library*.
25. R. Soame Jenyns. *Dictionary of National Biography*.
26. *Magdalen College Library*, MS 1084/3 184/535, 1913.
27. Ibid: MS 1084/4 184/545, 1914.
28. As the university did not confer degrees *in absentia*, Stewart Lockhart did not receive his degree until 1918, and Johnston in 1929. *University of Hong Kong, Calendar*, 1919 and 1930.
29. *Lockhart Papers*: Letter, 17 November 1917, *National Library of Scotland*.
30. Ibid: Letter, 24 September 1918.
31. The approach to Johnston and the

background to the offer can be built up from letters to Stewart Lockhart, 1918–20, in the *Lockhart Papers*. See also the Public Record Office, *Colonial Office Series*, 18353 521/20.

CHAPTER 3:

1. Tzu Hsi assumed the title *T'ai-huang-t'ai-hou* (Empress Grand Dowager) by Decree in the name of the infant Pu Yi, 15 November 1908. Because she lived in a palace in the western quarter of the Forbidden City she was also known as *Hsi T'ai-Hou* (Western Empress Dowager).
2. For the best assessment of Tzu Hsi's life and times to date, see Warner, M., *The Dragon Empress*.
3. Irons, Neville John, *The Last Emperor*, Chapter 1.
4. Bland, J.O.P. and Backhouse, E., *China Under the Empress Dowager.*
5. *Twilight in the Forbidden City*, Chapter IV.
6. Aisin-Gioro Pu Yi, *Journals.*
7. Ibid.
8. Ibid.
9. *Twilight in the Forbidden City*, Chapter VII.
10. General Chang Hsun wore the pig-tail queue in deference to the Ch'ing dynasty. The hairstyle had been introduced in the seventeenth century. He insisted his troops also adopted the style and his forces were dubbed the 'Pig-tail Army'. See, *Twilight in the Forbidden City.* Chapter X is given over to the 'autobiography' of Chang Hsun.
11. Aisin-Gioro Pu Yi, *Journals.*

CHAPTER 4

1. Public Record Office, *Colonial Office Series*, 18353 CO521/20.
2. J. & R.A. Robertson, Edinburgh. *Correspondence Files.*
3. In the year 1919–20 Johnston received £3,050. National Library of Scotland. *Lockhart Papers*: Letter, vol. 10.
4. *Twilight in the Forbidden City*, Chapter XII.
5. *Twilight in the Forbidden City*, Chapter XI.
6. Aisin-Gioro Pu Yi, *Journals.*
7. Irons, Neville John, *The Last Emperor*, Chapter 5.
8. Behr, Edward, *The Last Emperor*, Foreword.
9. Douglas, R.K., *Society in China.*
10. A commentary on the *Ch'un ch'iu* (Spring and Autumn Annals), a record of major events during the eponymous period 772–481 BC.
11. Mitamura, Taisuke, *Kangan: Sokkin Seiji no Kozo*, Chapter II.
12. Ibid.
13. *Twilight in the Forbidden City*, Chapter XI.
14. Aisin-Gioro Pu Yi, *Journals.*
15. National Library of Scotland. *Lockhart Papers*: Letter, 29 March 1919, vol. 10.

16. A translation of the *Li Chi* was prepared by Thomas Legge within the *Sacred Books of the East* (1885), which Johnston quotes in *Twilight in the Forbidden City*, Chapter XII.
17. Power, Brian, *The Puppet Emperor*. Estate of M.I. Johnston; Aisin-Gioro Pu Yi, *Journals*.
18. Sir James Stewart Lockhart resigned his post at Weiheiwei and left China in 1921, aged 63. He bought a house at Cresswell Gardens, off Brompton Road, South Kensington, London. He reciprocated Johnston's letters and sent him books and papers of Chinese academic interest. He became an elector at the School of Oriental Studies, University of London, and was later to be a key player in Johnston's appointment to the Chair of Chinese in 1931. Lockhart died on 26 February 1937.
19. Aisin-Gioro Pu Yi, *Journals*. In her article 'Imperial Tutor: Sir Reginald Fleming Johnston (1874–1938)' in *Country Life* (25 September 1986), Evelyn Battye notes that at Johnston's two-storied mansion at Peking – dubbed 'Johnston's Lodge' by Europeans – he included Pu Yi's future empress in his 'gentrification' dinner parties for Pu Yi, with the empress chaperoned by her American tutor Miss Isabel Ingram. See also: *Twilight in the Forbidden City*, Chapter XXI.
20. Aisin-Gioro Pu Yi, *Journals*. For Johnston's comments on Pu Yi's calligraphy see *Twilight in the Forbidden City*, Chapter XIV.
21. Letter from Johnston to Lord Li, 7 March 1919. National Library of Scotland. *Lockhart Papers*, vol. 10.
22. *Twilight in the Forbidden City*, Chapter XVII.
23. Magdalen College Library. Letter: Johnston to Sir Herbert Warren, 21 May 1923.
24. Behr, Edward, *The Last Emperor*, Chapter 7.
25. Magdalen College Library. Letter: Johnston to Sir Herbert Warren, 21 May 1923.

CHAPTER 5

1. *Twilight in the Forbidden City*, Chapter XII.
2. Magdalen College Library. Letter: Johnston to Sir Herbert Warren, 21 May 1923.
3. Aisin-Gioro Pu Yi, *Journals*.
4. *Twilight in the Forbidden City*, Chapter XVIII.
5. Ibid: Chapter XVIII. See also a letter to an anonymous correspondent, 8 June 1922.
6. Behr, Edward, *The Last Emperor*, Chapter 8.
7. *Moore Papers*.
8. Behr, Edward, *The Last Emperor*, Chapter 8. See also Johnston's articles in *The Times*, Jan/Apl, 1923.
9. *Twilight in the Forbidden City*, Chapter XIX.

10. The Estate of M.I. Johnston. Also National Library of Scotland. *Lockhart Papers*: Letter: 17 January 1923.
11. For a sequence of events see: Irons, Neville John, *The Last Emperor*, Chapter 7. In Johnston's own account of the event, *Twilight in the Forbidden City*, Chapter XX, he makes no mention of the Dutch Minister's name or legation.
12. National Library of Scotland, *Lockhart Papers*. Letter: 17 January 1923.
13. Ibid: Letter, 31 January 1923.
14. Ibid: Letter, 31 January 1924. Johnston taught the emperor and empress how to play tennis and cycle games.
15. For this and the sequence of events between 23 October and 5 November 1924, see *Twilight in the Forbidden City*, Chapter XXIII.
16. Aisin-Gioro Pu Yi, *Journals*.
17. Behr, Edward, *The Last Emperor*, Chapter 10.
18. *Twilight in the Forbidden City*, Chapter XXV.

CHAPTER 6

1. *Morrison Papers*: Letter, Johnston to Morrison from Wu T'ai Shen, 6 July 1908. As with so many foreign correspondents at the time, Morrison was also an early admirer of the Japanese, but was to become disillusioned by the advance of harsh militarism.
2. Ibid: Letter, Johnston to Morrison from Ta Chush SSu, 1 July 1915.
3. Irons, Neville John, *The Last Emperor*, Chapter 9.
4. *Twilight in the Forbidden City*, Epilogue. The British Minister, Sir Ronald Macleay was on leave at the time and the chargé d'affaires (Sir) Charles Michael Palairet (1882–1956) was acting in his absence.
5. Ibid.
6. Wood, Frances, *No Dogs and Not Many Chinese*, Chapter 15.
7. Trevor-Roper, Hugh, *Hermit of Peking*, Chapter 5.
8. See note 6.
9. Trevor-Roper, Hugh, *Hermit of Peking*, Chapter 11.
10. See note 4.
11. See note 4.
12. *Twilight in the Forbidden City*, Chapter XXII.
13. National Library of Scotland, *Lockhart Papers*. File, February 1925.
14. Ibid: Letter, Johnston to Stewart Lockhart, 28 February 1925.
15. He was really twenty by Chinese reckoning. In China a baby is aged one on the day of its birth.
16. Aisin-Gioro Pu Yi, *Journals*.
17. In his letters to friends and colleagues, Johnston continually bemoaned the fact that China was being treated so 'shamefully' by the

allies. In one letter he cites his 'rank treason' in castigating his own service department. *Morrison Papers*: Johnston to Morrison from Weiheiwei, 21 February 1913.

18. National Library of Scotland, *Lockhart Papers*. Letter, Johnston to Stewart Lockhart, 13 May 1927.
19. For an example of Johnston's forthright opinions see: *Morrison Papers*: Johnston to Morrison, 21 February 1913.
20. *Twilight in the Forbidden City*, Epilogue.
21. Behr, Edward, *The Last Emperor*, Chapter 12. Herein he quotes the memory of *The Times* correspondent Henry Woodhead.
22. National Library of Scotland, *Lockhart Papers*. Letter: Johnston to Stewart Lockhart, 21 August 1927, vol. 10a.
23. Ibid: Johnston to Stewart Lockhart, 3 March 1927 and 13 May 1927. See also minute on Johnston by Sir Miles Wedderburn Lampson (1880–1964), Minister at Peking: *Foreign Office Papers*, 228/3726/3. Lampson had scant regard for Johnston's opinions; see, for example, *Foreign Office Papers*, 228/4254/85 (51a).
24. The Estate of M.I. Johnston.
25. Originally called the *Genyosha* (Black Ocean Society), the *Kokuryukai* had been founded in 1881 by Kotaro Hiraoka, a wealthy *samurai* (warrior) nobleman, after the Sino-French War of 1883–5; it was organised to train and infiltrate secret agents into China. The *Kokuryukai* played a useful role in the Russo-Japanese War, 1904–5, and under leader Mitsuru Toyama deeply penetrated every layer of Japanese society. Many of the servants and attendants in the Cheng Garden were Black Ocean members.
26. Berg, Maxine, *A Woman of History: Eileen Power*.
27. *Shan-chu* – 'soul/spirit tablets' – set up to contain the divine inspiration or afflates of the dead. Johnston also set up tablets to the poet, engraver and mystic William Blake and the poet John Keats. *varia lectio*: Toynbee, Arnold J., *A Journey to China, or, Things which are Seen*, London, 1931.
28. Johnston, *Lion and Dragon in Northern China*, Chapter VIII. Johnston was an Associate Member of the Incorporated Society for Psychical Research from 1910, and a Member from 1930.
29. Girton College Archives, *Power Papers*. Letter: Power to the Cambridge don Gordon George Coulton, 23 December 1921.
30. *T'ao Yuan-ming*, or *T'ao Ch'ien* (365–427): civil servant who escaped to the land and became a rustic poet; *Po Chu-I* (772–846):

Governor of Hangchow, a great poet of the T'ang Dynasty; *Li Po*, or *Li T'ai po* (701–762): leading Taoist poet of the T'ang Dynasty.

31. Essay (imaginative) later published in *The Raven*. It appears in Eileen Power's 'Travel Diary', vol. III. See also Berg, *A Woman of History*.
32. National Library of Scotland, *Lockhart Papers*: Johnston to Stewart Lockhart, 14 October 1929 and 2 February 1930.
33. Roberts, R. Ellis, *Portrait of Stella Benson*.
34. *Twilight in the Forbidden City*, Epilogue.

CHAPTER 7

1. *Twilight in the Forbidden City*, Epilogue.
2. Ibid.
3. Ibid.
4. Behr, Edward, *The Last Emperor*, Chapter 14. When Johnston's book was published in 1934, the chapter bore a rather truncated version of what he had originally planned.
5. *Curtis Papers*, Letter, Johnston to Curtis, 17 June 1931.
6. Johnston was a member of The Atheneum; Thatched House; and Royal Societies Club, among others.
7. National Library of Scotland, *Lockhart Papers*: Johnston to Stewart Lockhart: Sequence 1 May, 15 November and 17 November 1917, vol. 10.
8. A seminal article on Johnston at the School of Oriental Studies giving background to the school and Johnston's career therein is to be found in Robert A. Bickers, '"Coolie work": Sir Reginald Johnston at the School of Oriental Studies, 1931–1937', *Journal of the Royal Asiatic Society*, Series 3, 5, 3 (1995), pp. 385–401.
9. National Library of Scotland, *Lockhart Papers*: Johnston to Stewart Lockhart, 15 August 1931.
10. Girton College Archives, *Power Papers*. Power to Margery Lois Garrett, 25 December 1930.
11. *Benson Papers*: Johnston to Stella Benson, 12 August 1931.
12. Berg, Maxine, *A Woman of History*.
13. *Twilight in the Forbidden City*, Notes; Introduction.
14. Markham, Sarah, 'Tutor to an Emperor'.
15. *Abbreviated Register of Sasines*, Dept of Administration, Argyll & Bute Council. 602: Lib 728. 240.
16. See note 8.
17. *Twilight in the Forbidden City*, Epilogue.

CHAPTER 8

1. *Street Directory*, 1936–40, Hove Library. In the article 'Scots Mandarin in the Forbidden City' in the *Glasgow Herald*, Saturday, 13 February 1988, Edna Robertson averred that Elizabeth Sparshott 'had

sought out [Johnston] after reading *Twilight in the Forbidden City*.'

2. Author's correspondence with Dr James Pitt-Payne. Elizabeth Sparshott lived at a flat in Oaklands Road, Bromley, before moving to the Sloane Nursing Home, Albemarle Road, Beckenham, Kent, where she died.
3. J. & R.A. Robertson, Edinburgh. *Correspondence File*, 1936.
4. Author's correspondence with the late Mrs George Forbes (Annie Mackenzie).
5. Scottish Record Office, Edinburgh. Ref: SC 51/34/23. pp 81–2, C 44972.
6. *Abbreviated Register of Sasines*, Dept of Administration, Argyll and Bute Council. 4434. (No. 6). 2 July 1938.
7. J. & R.A. Robertson, Edinburgh. *Correspondence File*, 1938.
8. *Holograph*: A document wholly written by the person from whom it proceeds. The problem, and the basis for Johnston's sister Noney's legal objection, was that the holograph had not been witnessed. In her fury at being left out of the will it seems that Noney would have challenged any will, and certainly caused unpleasantness with all who were concerned with it. See the Viscount Dunedin *et al*, *Encyclopaedia of Scottish Legal Styles*, vol. IV. Ch: Declarator (Green & Son, 1936).
9. Scottish Record Office: SC 51/32/100 pp. 57–60. Inventory of Sir Reginald Fleming Johnston's British Estates.
10. J. & R.A. Robertson, Edinburgh. *Correspondence File*, 1938. Specifically letter to Col. R.R. Butchart, 23 August 1938.
11. See note 1, article by Edna Robertson.
12. Irons, Neville John, *The Last Emperor*, Chapter 10.
13. *Record of the International Military Tribunal for the Far East*. P1. 180/Rb 238. General Service Administration File.
14. *Twilight in the Forbidden City*, translation of Preface. Johnston averred that the calligraphy (alone) was by Cheng Hsiao-hsu.
15. Ibid: Epilogue, date of meetings, 7–9 October 1931.
16. See note 13 and Brackman, A.C., *The Other Nuremberg*, Chapter 14.

EPILOGUE

1. For a more detailed examination of Pu Yi's last years see the authors quoted in the Bibliography, *viz*: Power, Behr, Irons and Brackman.
2. *Notice of a Special Pardon from the Supreme People's Court of the People's Republic of China*. Clause 1. 4 December 1959.
3. Aisin-Gioro Pu Yi, *Journals*.
4. Obituary, *The Times*, 12 June 1997.
5. See note 1, particularly the biographies by Power and Behr.

BIBLIOGRAPHY

I MANUSCRIPT SOURCES

Record of the International Military Tribunal for the Far East, National Archives and Records Service, Washington, DC, USA.

Manshukokushi Hensan Iinkai, Lists 18 Sept 1931–15 August 1945. National Diet Library, Tokyo.

Shogaikoku ni okeru joho kankei kancho chosa ikken, Checklists: China 1898–1945. Japanese Ministry of Foreign Affairs, Tokyo.

Power Papers, Girton College Archives, Cambridge University.

Morrison Papers, State Library of New South Wales, Australia.

Colonial Office Services and *Foreign Office Services*, Public Record Office, Kew, Richmond, Surrey.

Registers of Births, Marriages and Deaths, Scottish Record Office, Edinburgh.

Stewart Lockhart Papers, National Library of Scotland, Edinburgh.

Johnston Correspondence, Magdalen College Library and Archives, Oxford University.

Johnston Correspondence, J. & R.A. Robertson, WS, Edinburgh.

Curtis Papers, Bodleian Library, Oxford University.

Moore Papers, The Estate of Mrs C.M. Moore (Private Collection)

Johnston Papers, The Estate of M.I. Johnston (Private Collection)

II BOOKS BY THE EMPEROR AISIN-GIORO PU YI

Wo-ti ch'ien-pan-sheng. Appeared in English as *From Emperor to Citizen: the Autobiography of Aisin-Gioro Pu Yi* (Foreign Language Press, Beijing, 1964–5).

Kramer, Paul (ed.) *The Last Manchu: The Autobiography of Henry Pu Yi Last Emperor of China* (Weidenfeld & Nicolson, 1967).

III BOOKS BY SIR REGINALD FLEMING JOHNSTON

The Last Days of Theodoric the Ostrogoth (printed privately for Johnston by Blackwells of Oxford, 1904).

Account of a Journey in Shantung from Weiheiwei to the Tomb of Confucius (Weiheiwei Press, 1904).

Remarks on the Province of Shantung (Norohara & Co., 1904).

From Peking to Mandalay: A Journey from North China to Burma through Tibetan Ssuch'uan and Yunnan (John Murray, 1908).

Lion and Dragon in Northern China (John Murray, 1910).

A Chinese Appeal to Christendom Concerning Christian Missions (Watts & Co., 1911).

Buddhist China (John Murray, 1913).

Letters to a Missionary (Watts & Co., 1918).

Twilight in the Forbidden City (Victor Gollancz, 1934).

Confucianism and Modern China: The Lewis Fry Memorial Lectures 1933–4 (Victor Gollancz, 1934).

IV Books about Emperor Aisin-Gioro Pu Yi

Behr, Edward. *The Last Emperor* (Macdonald & Co., 1987).

Brackman, Arnold C. *The Last Emperor* (Scribner's, 1975).

— *The Prisoner of Peking* (Van Nostrand Reinhold, 1980).

Irons, Neville John. *The Last Emperor: The Life of the Hsuan-t'ung Emperor Aisin-Gioro P'u-yi 1906–1967* (House of Fans Ltd, 1983).

Power, Brian. *The Puppet Emperor: The Life of Pu Yi, Last Emperor of China* (Peter Owen, 1986).

V Background Reading

Airlie, Shiona. *Thistle and Bamboo: The Life and Times of Sir James Stewart Lockhart* (Oxford University Press (Hong Kong), 1989).

Alexander, Helen. *My Memories* (printed privately for the author by Laurence Gilbertson, Edinburgh, 1890).

Ashton-Gwatkin, F.T. *The British Foreign Service: A Discussion of the Development and Function of British Foreign Service* (Syracuse University Press, 1951).

Atwell, P. *British Mandarins and Chinese Reformers: the British Administration of Weiheiwei 1898–1930 and the Territory's Return to Chinese Rule* (Oxford University Press (Hong Kong), 1988).

Barnes, A.A.S. *On Active Service with the Chinese Regiment* (Grant Richards, 1902).

Bell, H.C.F. *Life of Palmerston* (London, 1936).

Benson, A.C. and Esher, Viscount. *The Letters of Queen Victoria: A Selection from Her Majesty's Correspondence* (John Murray, 1907).

Berg, Maxine. *A Woman of History: Eileen Power 1889–1940* (Cambridge University Press, 1996).

Bland, J.O.P. and Backhouse, E. *China Under the Empress Dowager* (Heinemann, 1910).

Bruce-Mitford, C.E. *The Territory of Wei-Hei-Wei* (Weiheiwei, 1902).

BIBLIOGRAPHY

Cheng, J.C. *Chinese Sources for the Taiping Rebellion, 1850–1864* (Hong Kong University Press, 1963).

Coates, P.D. *The China Consuls: British Consular Officers 1843–1943* (Oxford University Press, 1988).

Cohen, Paul A. *History in Three Keys: The Boxers as Event, Experience and Myth* (Columbia University Press, 1997).

Conroy, Hilary. *The Japanese Seizure of Korea* (London, 1960).

Couling, Samuel. *Encyclopaedia Sinica* (Kelly & Walsh, 1917).

Endacott, G.B. *A History of Hong Kong* (Oxford University Press, 1985).

Grant, Joy. *Stella Benson: A Biography* (Macmillan, 1987).

Heren, Louis, *et al. China's Three Thousand Years: The Story of a Great Civilization* (Times Newspapers Ltd, 1973).

Hurd, Douglas. *The Arrow War: an Anglo-Chinese Confusion 1856–1860* (William Collins, 1967).

Kent, Percy Horace. *The Passing of the Manchus* (Edward Arnold, 1912).

Kong Demao and Ke Lan. *House of Confucius* (Hodder & Stoughton, 1988).

Leslie, J.B. *Derry Clergy and Parishes* (privately published, Enniskillen, 1937).

Lo Hui-Min (ed.). *The Correspondence of G.E. Morrison* (Cambridge University Press, 1976).

McAleavy, David. *A Dream of Tartary* (George Allen & Unwin, 1963).

Martin, Christopher. *The Boxer Rebellion* (Abelard-Schuman, 1968).

Michie, Alexander. *The Englishman in China during the Victorian Era as demonstrated in the Career of Sir Rutherford Alcock KCB, DCL* (Blackwood, 1900).

Mitamura, Taisuke. *Kangan: Sokkin Seiji no Kozo* (Chuo Koron Sha, Tokyo, 1963).

Platt, D.C.M. *Cinderella Service: British Consuls Since 1825* (Longman, 1971).

Pope-Hennessy, James. *Half-Crown Colony* (Jonathan Cape, 1969).

Smith, Charles J. *Historic South Edinburgh* (Charles Skilton, 1978).

Trevor-Roper, Hugh. *Hermit of Peking: The Hidden Life of Sir Edmund Backhouse* (Macmillan, 1976).

Twitchett, D. and Fairbank, J.K. (eds) *The Cambridge History of China* (Cambridge University Press, 1978–80).

Warner, Marina. *The Dragon Empress* (Weidenfeld & Nicolson, 1971).

Waley, Arthur. *The Opium War Through Chinese Eyes* (Allen & Unwin, 1958).

Wood, Frances. *No Dogs and Not Many Chinese: Treaty Port Life in China, 1843–1943* (John Murray, 1998).

Woodhead, H.G.W. *A Journalist in China* (Hurst & Blackett, 1934).

Wright, Arnold. (ed) *Twentieth-Century Impressions of Hong Kong, Shanghai and Other Treaty Ports in China* (Lloyd's Great Britain Publishing Co., 1908).

INDEX

INDEX

INDEX